Little Gears of Time

Praise for *Little Gears of Time*

The passion in these poems both frightens and comforts me. What can we give our mothers to heal their wounds? What can we tell our daughters so that they turn their futures toward happiness? The answer is only what you already know: love, love, love, but it is a rainbow: never seek the same one twice. It is courage and hope that bend the bow and renew its dazzling, airy shape. This is a book that can strengthen generations.
— Sena Jeter Naslund, author of *Ahab's Wife*,
Four Spirits, and *Abundance,* among others

Only once in a generation, or perhaps a century, does an American poet succeed in recapturing the scale and scope of America as did Walt Whitman. Even more rarely does one give Whitman a run for his money. With her collection *Little Gears of Time* Susan Martinello has not only recaptured Whitman's scale and scope but has expanded Whitman's vision into the world of the feminine and made it relevant to America in the twenty-first century. Rarely does an elegant epic collection of this importance appear on the scene.

Like Whitman's *Leaves of Grass*, Martinello's collection is the most American book possible, a country of immigrants whose story is best told by those who were once outside it. A stunning evocation of the lives and experiences of six women, ranging from the early nineteenth century to the present day, Martinello's collection is a heart-breaking familial saga encapsulating the wide sweep of history and experience during most of the past two hundred years. Any collection of poetry that begins with a family tree is already filled with promise.

The collection could not be more relevant, given the fault lines of American life that are so exposed in contemporary life. Only through work like this one can the rifts that separate Americans be

healed. Let me borrow Emerson's words in response to Whitman's first edition of *Leaves of Grass* to characterize my response to *Little Gears of Time* - "I rubbed my eyes a little, to see if this sunbeam were no illusion; but the solid sense of the book is a sober certainty. It has the best merits, namely, of fortifying and encouraging."
    — Carlos Dews, Ph.D., M.F.A. writer and professor,
    Director of the Institute for Creative Writing and Literary
    Translation at John Cabot University in Rome, Italy

This breathtaking book expands the boundaries of what poetry can be by adeptly using persona, history, and drawings to explore multiple generations of women based on Martinello's family. One epigraph by Cokie Roberts asks, "So what is a woman's place? For most women, it's many places, different places at different times." By its capacious spirit and imagistic ingenuity, these poems allow the reader to feel the full truth of this statement. These are poems deftly crafted that are unsentimental yet aligned to the senses. A poetic tour de force!
    — Charlotte Pence, author of *Many Small Fires* (Foreword
    Reviews' IndieFab Book of the Year) and *Code,* and
    Director of the Stokes Center for Creative Writing at the
    University of South Alabama

Little Gears

of

Time

— Susan Martinello —

Little Gears of Time

Copyright © 2020 Susan Martinello
All rights reserved

Edited by Sue Brannan Walker
Book Design and Illustrations by Jenni Krchak
Author Photo by Diane Davis Photography

ISBN 978-0-942544-06-0
Library of Congress Control Number: 2019944137

Negative Capability Press
150 Du Rhu Drive, #2202
Mobile, Alabama 36608
(251)591-2922

www.negativecapabilitypress.org
facebook.com/negativecapabilitypress

For Mothers and Daughters —
Our stories forever intertwine.

Contents

Family Tree	vi
Introduction	1
In My Love, in My Song	5

PART I

Making Clothes for Lotte	11
Making Clothes for Lotte	12
Johannes, Listen	13
Papa's Little Spatz	14
A Dark Winding	16
Dealing	17
Dearest Ursula,	18
I walk up the ship's gangplank	19
I call this our once upon a time	21
Dear Papa,	22
All Those Mornings Ago—	25
Thanksgiving	27
Considering Liberty	28
Dear Papa,	29
At 3:00pm in her parlor	31
Old Enough	33
Das Neujahr	34
Taking Care of Baby	36
Taking Care of Baby	37
Ghost	39
Part I Notes	41

PART II

Penny Candy	47
Penny Candy	48

KLARA — MAGDA — AMELIA — RUTH — NORA — LARA

God's Curse	49
Mrs. S Gives after Mrs. S Takes Away	50
Dear Papa,	52
To my daughter Amelia I leave	54
Gift	56
My Grand Tour with Mrs. S	57
Follies	61
Finding William	62
One Last Burden	63
Early Daffodil	67
Tally	68
Part II Notes	69

PART III

Beach Glass	75
Beach Glass	76
Brownie Camera	77
Safely Married	78
Absence	79
Mother tells us who we are —	80
Reading Stone	81
Beacon	82
Another War	84
Scissor-bird	85
Chemistry	86
More Chemistry	87
Fingers Crossed	88
Honeymoon	91
Dear Mother,	92
Dear Ruth,	93
Part III Notes	94

PART IV

Reading Aloud	101
We Both Sewed	102
We Both Sewed	103
Reading Aloud	104
Humpty Dumpty	105
The Heart's Answering Echo	107
Milestones	109
Noon Air Raid Siren	110
Portuguese Blue	111
Until It Wasn't There	113
In Goodwill	114
The Dance	
Development	115
Stone	116
Questions for a Grandmother I Have Never Met	117
Coming Back	118
Barcelona Apollo	119
The Dance	
Variation	120
Adrift	121
How a Mother Bites Her Tongue	122
Home on Daddy's Island	124
Family Name	125
Potter's Field	127
I Am Not Good with Costumes, or,	
One-Woman Show with Tragic Flaw	128
Let's Hope It Lasts	130
So Close to Broken	133
Unspoken	134
Blessing	135
The L Word	137
Unzipped	139
Mom in a Once Familiar Place	140
Bead by Bead	141

Husband in Black and White	143
Souvenir	144
Part IV Notes	146

PART V

Adoption	153
Adoption	154
Ruth, In Memoriam	155
Sympathy Card from My First Grade Teacher	157
Love in the Time of Gardenias	158
Chopped spaghetti and mashed meatballs were my first foods.	159
Swiss	160
Cat Dreams	161
Logic	163
Doesn't Every Girl?	164
Laws of Geometry	166
Prom Magic	167
Second Chance Shop	168
My Roman life	169
Venus in the Eternal City	171
Opening the Green Paisley Odds and Ends Photo Album on a Visit Home	173
It's as if	175
Through the Lens of a Wedding	177
Bound for America	179
Wife-heart	180
Alpha and Omega	181
Untethered	182
The Sound of Her Name	183
His Word	184
Circling the Sea	185
Part V Notes	187

Vocabulary of Foreign Words 189
Acknowledgments 191
Appreciation 193

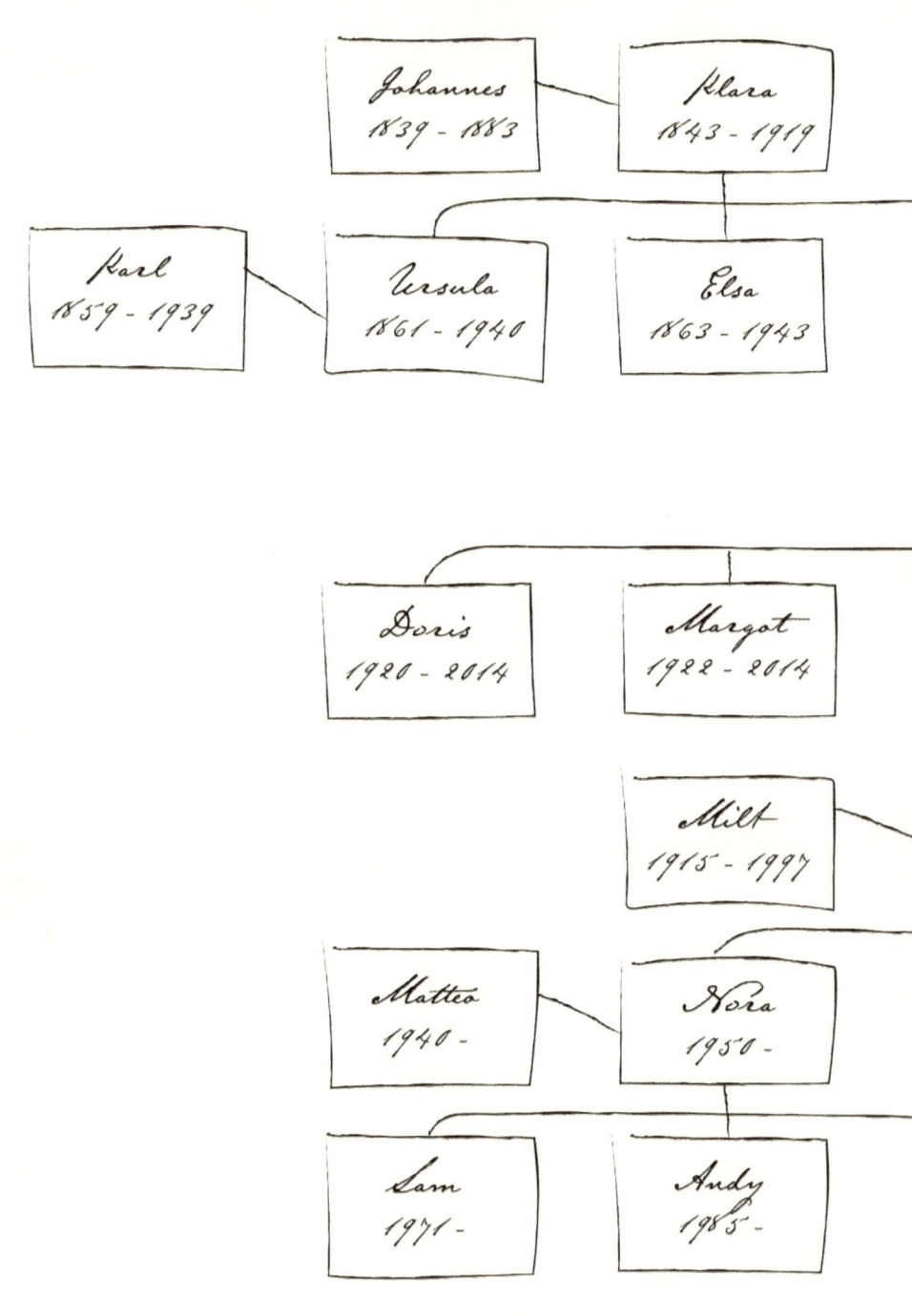

Family Tree

- **Magda** 1870 – 1909
  - **Amelia** 1892 – 1990 + **William** 1898 – 1975
    - **Eddie** 1928 – 2019
    - **Tommy** 1933 – 2005
    - **Ruth** 1924 – 1993
      - **Paul** 1952 –
      - **Danny** 1960 –
        - **Lara** 1987 – + **Pietro** 1982 –
          - **Nora** 2017 –

Introduction

Discover a time capsule. It doesn't contain much—gold pocket watch, breathy, long distance telephone voice, points of *t*'s and *p*'s in handwriting twining around the edge of letters, a handful of snapshots. Freshly baked bread provides swift transport for the imagination.

A woman's artifacts tick in my belly, drawing a time line forward and back from one woman to a chain of six, a family line of mothers and daughters. Their lives become a play needing a stage.

This is as close as I get to a photograph—wispy gray hair and the blue lapis beads of a necklace, their suggestions of wisdom. The face—ah—the crooked smile of yes and no, true and untrue, fact and fiction. Their story and our story.

Six bodies hold written in their cells not only their own reasons, but those of ancestors. People who left home and came to America from

> England, seeking religious freedom, 1635
> West Indies, following the father of her unborn child, 1858
> Azores Islands, escaping poverty, 1880
> Switzerland, a widow finding a home for her daughters, 1883
> Azores Islands, running away from a mean stepmother, 1900
> Italy, leaving a war-ravaged town, 1955
> Italy, looking for opportunity, 2015

Six women do the best they can—moving to a new country, living in a lighthouse, feeling lost in a river valley, discovering a new life and language. They speak of fathers and husbands, secrets, and, of course, mothers and daughters.

I lift the scalloped edge of my white apron, present the cast upon their stage:

> Klara, clear-sighted except with regards to
> her daughter Magda, a maiden, a Magdalene, single mother of
> Amelia, fated to the hard work implicit in the name.
> Her middle child, Ruth, honest and naive
> mother of Nora, who shines the light for
> daughter Lara, weaver of the laurel wreath.

They wear love like an undergarment—sometimes voicing it with a harsh word, sometimes with no word at all.

Fiction isn't memory.
But memory is fiction.

—Jane Gardam, *Crusoe's Daughter*

Klara
34 years old
Lucerne, Switzerland, 1877

In My Love, in My Song
— Friedrich Rücker, *In mienem Lieben, in mienem Lied!*

Late afternoon light teases shadows from kitchen corners
like fish darting in our pond. With a flick of my wrists,
I cast the worn white tablecloth like a net over the table.
It floats, brushes my arm with a shiver of memory—
my wedding day, a silk dress rustling over raised arms—
frees the whisper of waking dream. I see
my three daughters sitting in their accustomed places,
the blonde braids of the youngest long on her back.

But in the next moment, they are making room
for their daughters, who squeeze a bit for their daughters,
who scuff their chairs closer for their daughters.
We find more chairs, more room. Dear Mütter,
dead these five years, commands the table.
I tuck a stool next to me for my sister.
We pass around our favorite dishes, raise them
to inhale fragrant steam of dill and caraway. Even aromas
I don't recognize, I seem to remember. We laugh,
savoring foods we didn't know we craved.
We cry and hug over stories tasting
of foreign words. We know them as our own.

My tired husband comes in from the vineyard for supper
to find me smiling, still holding the tablecloth's daisied
edge. He notes the tilt of my head and asks what I hear.
I say the music of dust motes on late rays of sun.
He shakes his head.
Women.

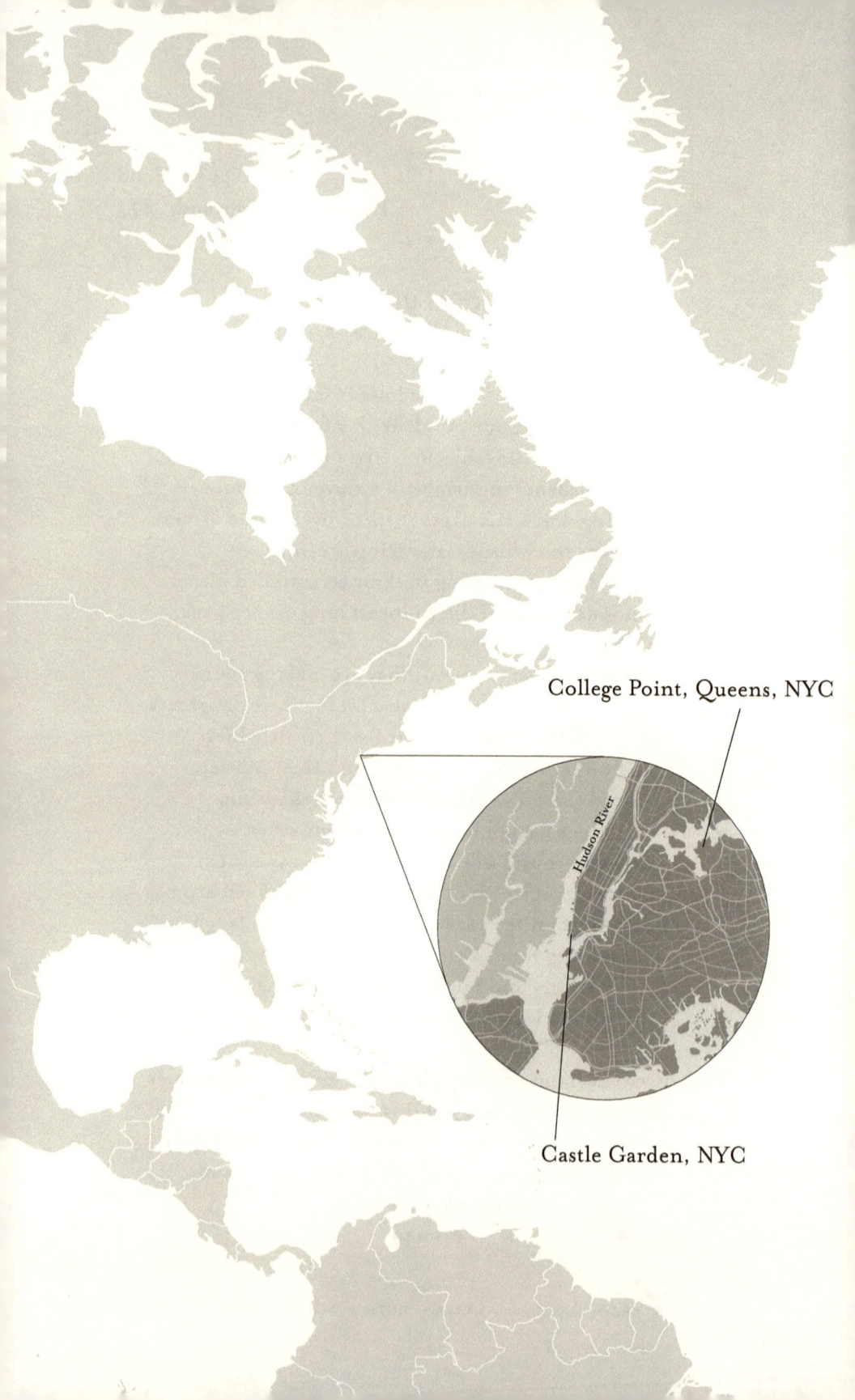

PART I

1878 - 1895

Bremen, Germany

Basel, Switzerland

Lucerne, Switzerland

She knows what she sees. She has her eyes in the right place.
— Johanna Spyri, *Heidi*

Swiss author Johanna Spyri (1827-1901) published *Heidi* in 1881. She began writing during the Franco-Prussian War to raise money for the Red Cross. The characters in her books face the widespread poverty, hunger, inhumane factory conditions of 19th century Switzerland. She was particularly concerned about orphaned children like Heidi, whose guardian Aunt Dete had to emigrate to make a better living. Some 330,000 Swiss would emigrate between 1850 and 1888, most to the United States.

Magda
8 years old
Lucerne, Switzerland, 1878

Making Clothes for Lotte

I dump Mama's basket of sewing scraps
on the kitchen table, make a rainbow.
My finger skips - ene - mene - miste -
from my red gingham to Elsa's green linen
to Mama's blue-flowered crepe and over again
until it ends on blue.
At the bottom of the basket I find
bits of lace that Elsa brings home.
Lotte will have a grown-up frock
this time. I help sew the seams.
Hemming is hard. Mama says
when I learn to take smaller stitches,
I can make a dress all by myself.
And then a bonnet
for the best doll in the world.

Klara
35 years old
Lucerne Switzerland, 1878

Making Clothes for Lotte

Magda spends hours dressing her doll
for tea parties. My Mäuschen, whose own dresses
are grass-stained at day's end, keeps the doll's clothes
neat in the small wooden trunk
where Lotte sleeps. While we sew, her unblinking
blue eyes gaze at us from where she sits, patient
in her kitchen chair. She approves equally
of every dress, sometimes seems partial to lace,
but always favors the ones with buttons sewed
by Magda. When I am alone in the house, I say
Lotte out loud in greeting, caress her china fingers.
How easily she could be broken.

Klara
37 years old
Lucerne, Switzerland, 1880

JOHANNES, LISTEN

Today five francs, last week three francs.
Insignificant sums—
a dress-length of calico,
an umbrella to replace the one
the wind blew inside out
for the last time.

I have never stood between you
and a Saturday night at the tavern—
your game of euchre,
a stein of beer.
But lately I am long in bed
when you stumble home,
pockets empty.

You dream a hand of jacks,
forget you're a good family man.
Wake up before you lose.

Magda
10 years old
Lucerne, Switzerland, 1880

Papa's Little Spatz

I flatten myself against the floor
of Papa's cart. He waves to Mama,
click-clicks to the horse.
Papa is good at helping me
get out of beating rugs.
When the cart stops in the vineyard,
I throw off my shoes and stockings.
The dew is cool. I run up and down
the rows of grapes. My braids bounce.
The grapes are getting sticky
like honey so I know
the harvest is near. Sure enough,
Papa cuts me the first bunch.

In the afternoon, Mama says
the September sun makes
the hands of her clock lazy.
I play in the shade of the courtyard
oak. I wish I was old enough
to climb it, to make a house
in its leaves like the little sparrow
Papa calls me.

At the end of the day,
Elsa comes home from weaving
webs of lace, spins big sister tales
on the bench beside me.
A wolf with a great shaggy head
watches from the edge of the forest,

leaps out, and gobbles up girls
lost in making daisy chains.
Papa gets back from the vineyard,
and I run into his warm arms.

Magda
13 years old
Lucerne, Switzerland, 1883

A Dark Winding

I storm out the kitchen door
to the courtyard. Mama says
it's time to wind my braids
around my head. I don't want
to be a hair-pinned fräulein.
Already long skirts tangle
in my legs when I run.

I call *Papa, Papa* into the dark,
where he feeds the horse,
lets the cows and goats out
of the barn so the sun can't get a start
on the day before he does.
I walk a wide circle around
the courtyard tree turned
Schwarze Mann
after sundown.

Something like sunlight catches
in the dark branches. I turn to look.
The Schwarze Mann holds me
with all his powers.
A white gleam lures me closer.
Sleeves. Hands? Brown pants.
Papa's boots. Yes, a shirt.
I look up. Mama runs out.
I am a scream
that cannot stop.

                                    Klara
                               40 years old
                        Lucerne, Switzerland, 1883

Dealing

The neighbor men cut you down
from the conspiring oak. They slip off the rope
knotted by your own hand, and the skin
on my neck feels raw. My lips
press your name into a thin line.
You threw down our lives
with a hand of cards.

My eyes are storm clouds over your coffin.
You crushed Magda like a field daisy
under the wheel of your cart,
and I don't know how
to set her growing straight again.
Take this wedding ring with you into the dark ground.
I make you no more promises.

The gates of the Catholic cemetery
will not open for you to abide with your parents.
Husband, on the long walk
to the common burial ground,
a gnawed bone on the side of the road
brings my first tears.

Ah, Johannes,
a joker is shuffling
my cities, countries, continents.
I will never again be held by chance
in the hand of any man.

Klara
40 years old
Lucerne, Switzerland, 1883

DEAREST URSULA,

Your letter has made up my mind.
We will come to you in America.
The new owners of the farm
invite us to stay as long as we need,
but my ears ring with Magda's shrieking.
In the courtyard, I squeeze my eyes shut
against your Papa's final image,
try to keep him seated on the bench
under that oak smoking his pipe,
sharpening his pruning tools.

Hearing German in the streets
will ease us in College Point[1],
just as the Schlummerlieder I used to sing
comforted your way to sleep.

Knowing that I will soon meet
my two grandchildren keeps my spirits up.
Taking over their nursery
won't inconvenience you for long, I trust.
Yes, I will be sure to pack
linens, blankets, whatever crockery I can.
Your sister Elsa will certainly find work
in the lace factory you suggest.

Klara
40 years old
Bremen, Germany, 1883

I WALK UP THE SHIP'S GANGPLANK

without my sister
who helped birth my daughters,
without the warmth of my black iron stove,
its kitchen corner where those daughters
played dolls,
copied letters,

without the tranquility
of our shaded courtyard ever again,
or delirium of ripe grapes at harvest,
or comfort of afternoon tea and knitting
with my sister,

without Magda's pet goat,
frequent forager in the kitchen,
or weekly prospect of market day,
even with skirt-flapping walks
when my mind was blown clear,
and I had all I could do
to keep my scarf
on my head,

without the first sip
of fresh November wine, or the secret spot
my sister and I shared for end of summer
mushrooming, or sweet spring meadows
where I lay and watched cloud pictures
float across the sky,

without the sewing table
my father made for me when I married,
without Mama's clock that presided in the parlor,
sold for passage

to America,
without the husband
who made me crazy with his cards,
the same man who wooed me
with his laughter.

Klara
40 years old
Castle Garden, New York, 1883

I CALL THIS OUR ONCE UPON A TIME

because our knight has fallen,
and we need rescue. Because
we are exhausted by loss,
on a ship of people crowded
with hope. Because we arrive
at a place called Castle Garden[2],
and what small family of Swiss women
wouldn't like a castle—
even one with a rank harbor for moat?
Because we pass through
great wooden doors into fable
where a scribe peers over his glasses,
looks hard at me before asking my name.
I hold my breath, stare
over his shoulder through the open door
behind him because I glimpse
the happy ending called America.

Magda
14 years old
New York, 1884

DEAR PAPA,

This stays with me: your heavy body
like a broken branch hanging
from the oak, the awful
crook of your neck. The stone
on my heart's grave
is moss-covered. If only
I could ride in a cart with you again.
Elsa says writing you a letter
is like sending a prayer.

Papa, when you bet the vineyard
and turned up a losing card,
you cut us loose from Switzerland.
We sailed for America, bound to Ursula,
the sister I barely remembered,
and to that point on a map called New York.
Elsa's fingers that send bobbins
twirling into lace found her work right away.
My plain hands are mistresses
of no particular craft.

Mama called on Mr. and Mrs. Schenk,
your old friends from home.
They own a brewery and live on a street
called Park Avenue in a mansion.
That kind lady took me on as her companion.
Mama and Elsa got a second floor
apartment near Ursula. I visit them
on Sundays. I am getting better at listening
and talking in turn at dinner,
also reading aloud to Mrs. S.

At monthly soirées, I practice *I am happy
to make your acquaintance* with the polite
offer of my hand to gentlemen. I want to run,
hide under your arm like I did
when men came to the farm
to buy wine.

Klara
41 years old
College Point, Queens, 1884

All Those Mornings Ago—

Mama introduced me to the harsh grasp of the corset,
encouraged me into the crinoline's cage,
dressed it with three layers of petticoats.
From Oma came the lengths of silk, color of wild grapes,
for my wedding dress. My sister Gertrud, a married woman
of one year, smiled as she fastened the buttons
of the tight-fitting bodice with a crochet hook.
My arms, raised like wings
in their wide sleeves, would not lift me in flight.

Instead, the skirt was lifted over my head
and sank around me with a muffled sigh.
Gertrud was quick to check the heavy braids
she had woven and wound at my nape.
My palms obsessed over the crinoline's bony hips.
My fingers traced the damask stripes, up and down,
dull and shiny, like the grapes' bloom.
I could not see myself
in the looking glass Mama offered.

Papa put my untried right hand
into Johannes' callused one. I feared
my other hand, free to fidget with the velvet bow
at my waist, would betray me
when he slipped the ring on my finger.
But standing before Johannes, I found myself
in the crinkle of laughter in his eyes.

With years, the reflection dimmed
as marriage wove our wills
like narrow damask stripes. I altered
my wedding dress until it wouldn't take another
stitch, wore it to know my own grain,
rough and smooth, next to my skin.

Today in my new country,
on the first anniversary of his death,
I wear it in mourning
for all that never was.

Magda
14 years old
College Point, Queens, 1884

THANKSGIVING

Mrs. S tried to explain this holiday. We must
not be Swiss anymore, but Americans.
She told of the brave Pilgrims.
We come here refugees from sorrow, huddle
in a town of Germans. But the shapes
of our German words float by our neighbors,
cherry blossoms in a stand of oaks.

Sauerbraten and spätzli steam
at the center of our table. No turkey.
Mama refuses to cook that savage fowl,
which is fine with Elsa and me.
The sauce of cranberry Mrs. S sends
tastes of bitterness.

Do we feel thankful?
Elsa works in a lace factory
where cotton dust thickens the air
like porridge. Mama cannot step outside
her second floor apartment to pick dill.
I do not live with Mama.

I would be thankful to hear Papa call me
his little Spatz, thankful not to be too old
for my doll Lotte, thankful to watch
how Mama sews on buttons.
Would it be unseemly to give thanks
for pumpkin pie?

Magda
16 years old
Battery Park, New York, 1886

Considering Liberty

I stand
near the castle
of my American beginning
with Mrs. S, who trains me
in service to her days.
I am sixteen years old,
and we have come
for the dedication
of Miss Liberty.
Newly assembled,
she eyes us
from her cement mount
in the harbor.
My mistress remembers
her copper arm
on display in Madison Square Park,
like the limb of a giantess
from Brothers Grimm.
Passers-by craned their necks
at her gleaming torch.
For six years she reached
as if from deep in the earth
to the sky.
I close my eyes.
Buried alive.

Magda
21 years old
New York, 1891

Dear Papa,

The days tick by without you.
I have settled into a routine
with Mrs. S—afternoons of paying calls
or keeping At Homes[3],
learning needlework, answering letters. My writing
is much improved. I must write to you again,
though these words
are no prayer.

On a January afternoon, a visitor from Basel
arrived at the S's door. His Kaiser
mustache, its scent of Bay Rum when he bowed.
Oh, Papa.
My fingers forgot how to count
as Mrs. S ticked off the languages
that roll from his tongue in pursuit
of business. He held me with eyes
like yours, Papa.
Dark wizards.

I have been careful to make polite
conversation, just as Mrs. S has taught me.
When he isn't seeing to his business affairs,
he entertains us with stories of Zurich,
Berlin, Paris over tea in bone china cups
you can almost see through. He has begun
to take me on strolls in the park,
obeying Mrs. S's firm pointer
on her watch.

I'm finding it easy to forget
her other teaching, namely, that a young lady
should allow a gentleman's kiss only
on the hand or forehead, at most a cheek.
That such a kiss should be
delicate.

Magda
21 years old
New York, 1891

At 3:00pm in her parlor

Mrs. S convenes us,
Mama, Elsa, Ursula, and me.
I never knew the parlor chairs
to be so hard. Ursula hisses in my ear,
*So, Mama's favorite has fallen
and finds herself in a most adult pickle.*
Showing off her English.
I get the meaning.

Heads turn.
The businessman from Basel
enters the room. Eyes shift
to the gold ring on his finger.
He bows low, takes a seat by the door.
My hands keep smoothing the dress
across my lap. I want to run back
to Papa's arbors of purple grapes,
my dirndl muddy, braids flying.

Mama's mouth jumbles her words,
can't seem to find one to start.
Ursula clears her throat, assumes
her wife-of-a-factory-manager voice.
My sister bears the weight of this commerce.
In this moment, I know
she will not help me.

They agree
he remain bound by his wedding band.
I hear the words *leave New York at once.*
Did someone say *never welcome
in this house again?* Ursula demands
he seal this business with $5,000
on the unborn child.

No amount can cover
mutters Mrs. S.
Magda may stay on
as my housekeeper.

Magda
21 years old
New York, 1891

Old Enough

A stranger's brown eyes stare back
from the mirror. My straight back,
my proud neck, my lips' curve—all gone
with my heart to Basel. The elms
once whispered his name outside my window.
Now those syllables are raised
in a shutter-battering gale
like Mama shouting at Papa over cards.
The fruit of our passion, brought to light,
ripens. I used to think love was sweet
like the grapes from Papa's hands. Instead
I am tangled in a thicket of briars.
Papa tried to teach me about grapes
on the vine: too much rain makes mildew,
too much heat shrivels, too much cold withers.
He practiced the marriage of good grape scion
to strong root. I am neither good nor strong
and am only half. Every day I clean,
and on my knees anoint walnut furniture with oil.
Mrs. S sprinkles the name of his wife
like salt. When I think I will die, I know
I am old enough to climb Papa's tree.
Only the thimbleful of child
taken root in me
grounds my feet.

Klara
49 years old
College Point, Queens, 1892

Das Neujahr

Dear Gertrud,

A cardinal lights on my snowy window ledge
this eve of the new year. All jaunty brilliance
in the sun, he scolds me, sitting inside
dull with cares. Masked magician, he wings me back
to my Lucerne kitchen where I scattered seed
outside the window for a similar caller.

But I am far away, dear sister, reader
of my soul. I felt settled into our new life.
Magda had begun to look light-filled. I thought,
the darkness of finding her father is leaving her.
You would have recognized the Basel gentleman's sway,
that base friend of Mrs. S. When he returned
to his family, it was like Johannes' death all over.
Magda's nine months lacked only black clothes,
shrouded mirrors. Whenever I see Mrs. S,
she is careful to remind me that she
will not cast the first stone.

The night following Amelia's birth, I dreamed
she stitched her mother's sin
onto her own little sleeve. I woke up
thinking, *Born to a life of hard work,*
as her name bespeaks.

Ach! A black blot—the flutter of my hand
as the cardinal leaped to wing.
On the ledge, his red calling card.
A thing of wonder, like the freckle
under Amelia's chin.

Magda
23 years old
College Point, Queens, 1893

Taking Care of Baby

Three sweet, sleepless months at Mama's,
feeding and bathing little Amelia,
falling into her brown eyes. Then Mrs. S poked a hole
in our heaven with daily notes about taking up
my housekeeping duties. She arrived on our doorstep
to insist, suggesting I bring Amelia with me. It was a trick.
From the first she couldn't stand Amelia's cries.
So I have to leave her with Mama and Elsa. Each Monday
morning I sob my way into the city. How many diapers
I would gladly scrub instead of floors. On the weekends
Mama cluck-clucks that I am spoiling Amelia
with my coddling. I try to get enough of her delicious
skin against my cheek to last me all week.
Instead Amelia spoils me with love. She has saved
her first wobbly steps
for me.

Klara
50 years old
College Point, New York, 1893

Taking Care of Baby

Dear Gertrud,

Thank you for your wishes on my fiftieth year.
You are right—babies tire us at our age. I do not feel spry
of late. The long brown braid wound around my head,
that you always called my halo, is graying and thin. Now
that Amelia is toddling about, I have to take care
where I put my feet. Not a moment's repose. I can barely
get plates on the table for Elsa's return from work.
You should see how Elsa glows when she opens the door
and catches up her little niece in her arms. In truth, Amelia
brings warmth to these old cheeks, too. Songs swell
in my throat that I haven't sung since our mushrooming
afternoons, our sisterly harmonizing among the oaks.
When Friday comes for your two nieces here,
one reclaims the verses, while the other
can only offer a chorus.

Magda
25 years old
New York, 1895

Ghost

I like to pretend our gentleman from Basel
is with us upstairs still. On my way
to set out breakfast for Mrs. S,
I glance up the stairway, watch him descend
for his strong morning kaffee.
He carries himself with unflinching
straightness, his suit proper. When his eyes
speak freely of last night, I must cast down
my own answering eyes.

After setting down bucket and mop
on the marble floor of the foyer,
I pause to view myself mid-way on the stairs
in my wedding gown of pink satin,
that pink which is nearly peach. He said it heightened
my complexion so. Or, if I am feeling grand,
I wear white satin and lace
like Queen Victoria[4].

Dust rag in hand, I approach the staircase
to polish the balustrade. The ornate oak
is a forest of desolation. I swing around
to the front door, to the final image
of his back framed in light,
his voice, *I must be dead to you now
and you dead to me.*

I pressed his first kiss
into a white handkerchief hemmed
with lace, hid it in the back of a drawer.
Now I press it to my eyes.
Tears do not slake
the ghost of passion.

Part I Notes

1. *Dearest Ursula*
Ursula lives in College Point, Queens. In 1854 the German-American industrialist Conrad Poppenhusen expanded his Brooklyn manufacturing of hard rubber goods to College Point. The small farming town became a factory town primarily for his workers, most of them also German immigrants.

2. *I call this our once upon a time*
Predating Ellis Island, Castle Garden, or Castle Clinton, was America's first immigration station, welcoming over 8 million people from 1855 to 1890. It is located in Battery Park, New York City.

3. *Dear Papa*
The calling card, an indispensable accessory to fashionable, upper class life in Britain, Europe, and the eastern United States during the 19th and early 20th centuries, often displayed the day a lady would be At Home to receive visitors.
Calling with a card at the right time and in favorable circumstances could lead to an invitation to visit. These visits were strictly formalized as well, usually consisting of twenty minutes of polite conversation and allowed only during set times in the late morning or early afternoon. After a call was made, a return call was to be expected and the process continued.

4. *Ghost*
Queen Victoria set the modern fashion of white wedding gowns, though white was sometimes worn by nobles. In her case, she wore white to make a political statement of her duties as Queen, and also as a practical and patriotic gesture. The dress had a lace skirt, which she chose to support and stimulate the handmade lace artisans in a newly industrializing England. The rest of the dress was a vehicle for the lace.

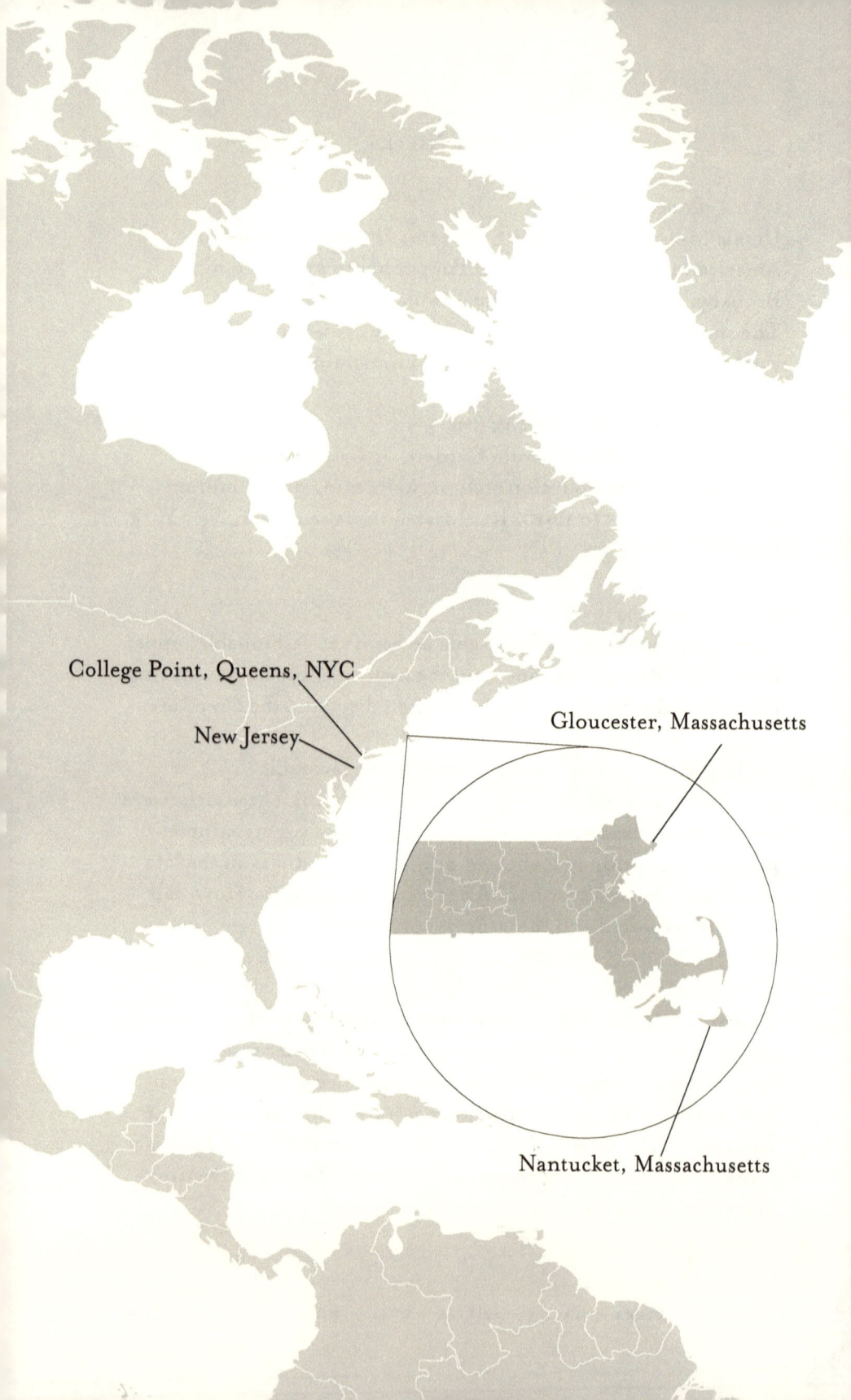

PART II

1898 –1927

Cologne, Germany
Le Havre, France
Basel, Switzerland
Lucerne, Switzerland
Paris, France
Venice, Italy
Milan, Italy
Pisa, Italy
Naples, Italy
Florence, Italy
Rome, Italy

Aviation offered such fun as crossing the continent in planes large and small, trying the whirling rotors of an autogiro, making record flights. With these activities came opportunity to know women everywhere who shared my conviction that there is so much women can do in the modern world and should be permitted to do irrespective of their sex.
— Amelia Earhart

Amelia Earhart, (1897-1937) was the first woman pilot to make a transatlantic flight. She was an early supporter of the Equal Rights Amendment.

Amelia
6 years old
College Point, Queens, 1898

Penny Candy

I look at the clock   run to the window
stretch my eyes   toward the station.
My feet are jumpy   every Friday afternoon
when Mama comes home.
I make out her brown coat   run
down the stairs   jump into her arms.
We can't even breathe   we are so happy.
She says   *What a lovely afternoon!*   I always answer
Let's buy some penny candy!   We walk to the corner store
hand in hand.   I pick my favorites
and two Tootsie Rolls[5]
for her.

Magda
28 years old
College Point, Queens, 1898

Penny Candy

The hands of the clock plod
towards four before I can dash
for the train. All the way home
the tracks jiggle-joggle me between
pain of distance and joy of nearing.
Buying a five-cent bag of candy
with Amelia gets me through the first
minutes. On the way back from the store
she tells me how she hates
arithmetic, how the girl who shares
her desk splattered ink on her new dress,
what Grossmutter has prepared for supper.
We pass the brown sack back and forth.
The words tumbling from her lips
and the melting on my tongue
are of the same sweetness. She
knows my favorite candies.
She is mine.

Amelia
13 years old
New Jersey, 1905

God's Curse

When Grossmutter's blue eyes   turn to frost
I am in for a talking-to   that doesn't end.
At finishing school   where Mrs. S has sent me
the sisters spare their words.   This morning I wake
to find blotches   the color of Mama's carnelian ring
on my white night gown.   The dormitory startles at my cries.
Girls come running   collapse in knowing giggles.
Sister Joseph takes me to the infirmary
tells me it is God's own curse   from the beginning of time.
Grossmutter's voice cursing a man   my first memory.

Sister makes me promise   to name this shame aloud to my mama.
I have learned here that Papas   turn from the unspeakable
send their daughters gloves and toffees.   I have learned to say
my papa died before I was born.   At home I plague Grossmutter
wave my long fingers   *Look, I have his hands!*

She makes me vow   to bury my father's name in silence.
In nightmares   of Tante Elsa's girl-eating wolves
I shout his name   at the man with a wolf's head.

Magda
35 years old
New York, 1905

Mrs. S Gives after Mrs. S Takes Away

No more moping about, Magda.
But Mrs. S, what joy do I have
with Amelia sent away?
Think of her rubbing elbows
with all those girls from good
families. Take joy in that.
Does she really need finishing school?
Formation of our proper young lady.
But why New Jersey?
We've been over that.
Aren't there girls of good families
over on Madison Avenue
at the Convent of the Sacred Heart?
I've thought it over.
What you need is a bicycle.
A bicycle?
They're all the rage.
Even my friend Violet's daughter rides one
in Central Park. Fresh air—a world of good.
Walking suits me fine.
Come out to the porch.
Here, look—latest model.
But I don't know how to ride.
Violet's daughter comes tomorrow.
Easy as pie, she says.

That's how I come to pedal around New York,
mousey wisps escaping my peacock blue hat.
I pump hard up my old hills,
coast down in fledgling flight.
As my grip on the handlebars loosens,
I wave at folks paused in doorways.
Still, my balance teeters
from smile to smile.

Magda
36 years old
New York, 1906

Dear Papa,

Remember how I used to write to you
in heaven? Tonight
the stars with their flickering
language of light spoke to me.
Mrs. S pointed into the night sky
at the Big Dipper—our Grosser Wagon.
I saw you then driving your horse and cart
around the vineyard, just as clearly
as Boötes drives the Great Cart
around the North Star. With a glimmer-flick
of reins, the heavenly cart driver
urged me to write again.

I see the Schwarze Mann
in the broad limbs of every oak.
He took hold of my soul
when you were loosed from his grasp.
I do not write to blame you,
but to say I still love you more than anyone.
You may say that mine
is a child's affection, but my love
is constant as Boötes.

I have never stopped asking, who
would kill himself over a game?
Mama's lips will not open around the word
kneipe, or even the English *tavern*.

I was blind to that rival for your attentions,
never questioning I was your only heart
as you were mine.

I failed to give my daughter a Papa
to love her. On a night such as this, blame
may flame up inside her. She may throw back
her head and cry out to the heavens.
But I have faith that from a few blinking stars
she will draw a constellation of compassion
around me. Tonight I feel sorry for you,
my own Papa. You didn't trust
we would forgive you. Or were you afraid
the weight of forgiveness would tip your cart,
tumble you from our heaven?

Magda
39 years old
New York, 1909

To my daughter Amelia I leave

the gold cross and chain at my neck,
the tiny crucified Christ
consumed by my fingers;
one silver hand mirror,
never as clear as the reflection
in my sister Elsa's eyes;
one carnelian ring, fleshly omen
taken by my father at euchre;
one trinket box with porcelain flowers,
Mama's gift
from fields of childhood;
one wash basin and pitcher painted with wild roses,
its fine brushwork of thorns with me
this eighteen-year duration;
one cameo of determined profile
I gaze upon
when courage runs out;
her lace christening gown
made by her Aunt Elsa,
never worn in a church;
one silver baby spoon with her initials,
gift of Mrs. S,
never lifted to her mouth;
one pair of pearl earrings,
loyal promise of her father,
never worn;
one album of family photographs
in the new world,
absent her Grossvater Johannes;

one headless china doll,
dropped the morning
I found him;
one photograph of her father and a lock of his hair,
sewn into a satin pouch,
my scapular;
seventy-seven dollars saved
to make a home for us[6].
Never enough.

                                              Amelia
                                           18 years old
                                          New York, 1910

GIFT

Mrs. S pins her birthday gift to my dress   her fingers fumble.
I flinch   a scarlet bud blooms.
Mama's fingers clasp their dark rest   bone on bone.
On the new gold watch   my initials entwine.
Where do they begin   or end   their deceit?

I duck into the small parlor   my party frock swirling
sink to the sofa.   This dress   against all mourning for Mama
ordered in sky-blue.   Ten years ago   I was told to sit still
on this sofa   but crawled under a chair   to grab a penny.
Voices stormed against the closed door   Grossmutter and Tante's voices
Mama and Mrs. S's.   I squeezed a birthday wish
from that penny   bought Mama a few more years
before Mrs. S   sent me away to school.

This evening   the pleasure of Grossmutter and Tante's company
is not requested.   Mrs. S strides about the great hall
broad swaths of emerald silk   orders floating in her wake
orders Mama used to satisfy.   I smooth my dress.   Taffeta sighs.
Oh   the penance Mama paid   each year of my eighteen.
Mrs. S sails in   plucks me back.   Arm-in-arm we sail out
to clink toasts   *to our dear Amelia.*
Sharp bubbles of champagne   sting my throat
like words of gratitude.

Amelia
18 years old
Europe, April - June, 1911

My Grand Tour[7] with Mrs. S

On the Friedrich der Grosser

Steamer trunks make a hollow sound rolling up the gangplank—
echo in my heart. My own trunk—fully furnished by Mrs. S
with daily frocks and dinner gowns—stands in my cabin
as though it belongs.

Ten seasick days from New York—the waters calm—as we pass
through the Strait of Gibraltar. I see at my first dinner—that claim
has been made on the company of several handsome beaux.

Naples

Worn planks of dock accept my unsteady steps—a new role:
Mrs. S's adopted daughter. I discover she carries letters
of introduction for every city—here the Conte and Contessa
send tickets for their box—at the gilded opera house of San Carlo.
Had they cared to join us—they would have had little to report
of me. I slept through it.

Rome

We walk up and down the naves of dark churches—buy
illumination to view paintings—only Saint Peter's is full of light.
Pope Pius X says Mass—blesses us and the holy objects
we bring—Mama's rosary tucked into my purse.
We tramp all around Rome—ancient ruins alive
with vines. In the Forum—I lose Mama's face
for a moment—among the fallen columns—shards of marble
like bone splayed along the Sacred Way.

Florence

The carriage driver drops us at our hotel. From my balcony
late afternoon sun paints the city with honey—sweeter
than the light in Rome. Mrs. S—unremitting in my education
declares—the Uffizi first thing in the morning.

Da Vinci's *Annunciation* captivates me—in my gaze
the face of Mary—becomes Mama's haloed face.
By day's end, my feet refuse—even one more gallery. Outside
I cannot raise my eyes to the David.
What would Mama think? My back to him—I take in the city.
The gold pin Mrs. S buys me on the Ponte Vecchio—
useless to hold together—the tear in my heart.

Pisa

My slant life seems—for the first time normal.

Venice

With canals threading around us—like a web—we take a strong
coffee in St. Mark's Square. In the night—I dreamt of Desdemona
haunting the alleyways. In crystal clear day—I hurry across
the Bridge of Sighs so I won't hear—Mama's whispers.
The Italian sun leaves—no shadowed corner where I can hide
from her—or avoid facing myself—the proper lady's companion
taking her place. Mrs. S devised her plan long before
I came into the world.

Milan

All streets lead to the monstrous Duomo.
Outside we need opera glasses to see—gargoyles.
Inside Mrs. S insists on seeing San Carlo—his remains.
A few lire in the sacristan's palm—a metal blind rises
like a magician's curtain—reveals a blackened corpse.
Oh—is this what Mama will look like? Sparkling jewels
surround the moldering saint—he glitters. I want to look
away—my eyes will not obey.

Through the Alps into Switzerland

A few days at Lake Como—villas seem painted
onto the hills. To think of ancient Romans—mesmerized
by the same reflecting blues—deep water—mountains—sky.
Another train—we chug into the Gotthard Tunnel. I fear
I will never see the sun again—finally snow-covered
peaks—dazzle. At the next station—Deutsch flooding
the corridor outside our compartment—gabble
of cherished ghosts. This diary—this scribbling—steadies
my anticipation of Lucerne—one Swiss farm causes
more excitement than—all of Italy's wonders.

At Last Lucerne

We leave our Tour group—ah—the pilgrimage to Mama's home.
On the bumpy coach ride, I look at everything—see nothing.
The plump hausfrau invites us in. I take my kaffee und kuchen
near Grossmutter's storied stove. Outside—the courtyard oak
stands less tall—less broad—than Mama's telling—but spreads
a chilly shade. A shiver—imagining Grossvater's hanging body—
shadow of a broken branch. I step quickly into the sun—nearer
the red-cheeked farmer smoking a pipe—worn to his palm. His
wife takes from her apron pocket—a gingham bonnet found under
the stove when they first moved in—too small for a baby.
So small—it escaped Grossmutter's sharp eyes
when she took Mama and Tante Elsa away to America.
Reminder to a young farm wife—of how she came to live here.
A child's uneven stitches still hold. Bonnet for Mama's doll Lotte.

Basel

Mrs. S makes an abrupt announcement—bank business here.
My father—the un-gentleman from Basel—rises, towers
higher than the Milan Duomo. In the Bahnhof—that rivals
Grand Central Station—all the gentlemen wear his face.
Strolling along the street with Mrs. S—I want to ask
Is that him?—Shout—*Is that him?*—Scream—*Is that him?*
She never mentions his name—he is not part of our itinerary.

Up the Rhine to Cologne

Days of diary pages, destination heading—*Father*—flow
like the Rhine—blank on the surface. Cologne—the Cathedral's
twin spires break through my daze. In the oldest part of the choir
I am stopped—wood carving on a misericord—girl doing
a handstand—skirt modestly draped over bent legs—looks out
with knowing eyes. I see that being upside down doesn't get
any better—or any worse—after six centuries.

Paris

We rejoin our Tour group at Versailles—Hall of Mirrors—hundreds
of solitary Amelia's—stretching as far as my eye can see
make me feel faint. Mrs. S declares—the Folies Bergère cabaret—
just the thing to revive my spirits. I am ashamed to say—it beats
everything I have seen.

Le Havre

Our ship looms—with the certainty—I shall never come back.
I fell on the childish knee of hope in Basel—go home
with a grown-up scar.

Amelia
24 years old
New York, 1916

Follies

Daily I wear the watch from Mrs. S   pinned or pendant
or pocketed   the slide chain long   or doubled around my neck.
No matter the trick   it ties me   to long afternoons with Mrs. S
in crewelwork   or reading aloud   news of the War
from *The Staats-Zeitung*[8].

With Mama a saint in heaven   I beg Mrs. S   let me join
the good Sisters of St. Joseph who schooled me.
A nun?   She almost spits the word.
After all I have spent raising you   to a respectable station?
You are nothing outside this house.   The young man who used to call
comes no more.   I understand.   She has strung what she calls
my   unsavory birth   around my neck.

The convent can be my only home now.   But Mother Superior
prays I seek God's guidance   toward some other vocation.
I do.   He seems to say   a children's nurse.
The S's door slams behind me.
I square my shoulders   on Tante Ursula's front stoop.
She helps me enter hospital training.

The nuns taught me to speak High German   to play the piano
but not   to comprehend the microscopic follies of biology.
When kind Dr. H says his daughter Ellie   needs a governess
I can only accept.

The gold watch   ticks on my bosom   like the time bomb
I read about in the newspaper.   I am homeless
motherless   childless.

Amelia
26 years old
New York, 1918

Finding William

What I see —
eyes blue as the Bay of Naples   lock of black hair
high forehead   shy grin.   A tall sailor tosses back Ellie's ball.
The red demon rolled over matted brown leaves in Central Park
over the curb   into his hands.   The Great War is over
sky less drab.   In my mind   the waves calm enough
to thank him.   Dear Ellie engages him in a game of catch
that lock of hair   that grin   loosed.

What I hear —
just *off a battleship*   waiting for *discharge papers*.   *Yes* to see
New York with me.   *Noisy, crowded*   (he did not witness
the victory celebration).   His intake of breath
at the eerie pyramid of captured German helmets.
Our footsteps into Grand Central Station.
His head-thrown-back declaration: *almost as big as the sky and ocean
around Nantucket Island*   echoes   *like waves breaking on the beach.*
Down   down into the new subway's hush   the train's
clacking arrival   wordless racket to the next stop.   Back
on the sidewalk   *breached like whales.*   St. Patrick's
a sand castle   each steeple *a slurry of drippings.*

What I know —
inside the cathedral   November sun slanting through
Lady Chapel windows   stains his face blue   jacket red
hands yellow.   I almost laugh out loud   in that sacred space.
He does not know about me.   The grapevine
of New York society   will not twine around him.

Klara
76 years old
College Point, New York, 1919

One Last Burden

Amelia, meine Schatz,

Elsa pleaded with me not to leave the house
with the Influenza[9] still about. I insisted on taking
a few of your old frocks to young Frau Hess. The fever
came on last night. I will not survive the Spanish Curse.
My weak fingers fret the lace wrist of my nightgown
with the urgency of my thoughts. Patient Elsa pens my words.

The weight of seventy-six years is lifting from my body.
Dreams of Johannes and Magda come more and more vivid.
Your sweet mama lived in a dream of another kind, trapped
in the shadow of her father. You were the only light
to filter through the leaves of the death tree,
the dapple on our days.

My child, keep walking away from your mama's darkness.
Your own will be enough to drag behind you.
I applaud your leaving Mrs. S. She came to our aid
in a difficult time, but she would have kept you
on the short leash of shame
until there was no way out.

Your mother was a trusting soul, your father a capable man—
though you know my opinion of his behavior.
Their noble traits flower in you.
Use the money your father left
to build a good life
with your young man.

Amelia, I have one last burden to put down
before I can rest. After your mother's death, Mrs. S received
a letter from your father. We determined
it would only upset you,
so we burned the letter unread. But that's not all. He sent
a gold watch for your eighteenth birthday.
Mrs. S decided it would best be a gift from her.

And so it was.
Find peace knowing
your father kept you in his heart.

Amelia
27 years old
Nantucket, Massachusetts, 1919

Early Daffodil

Feeling so fine a bride   in my pale yellow silk
last worn in Paris   with Mrs. S   God bless her.
I try   to think charitable thoughts.
Before the war   its high neck and long sleeves
caused fashionable fans to flick open   covering
smiles among ladies in décolleté   caused
gentlemen to consult   their pocket watches.
This morning I enter a church   William's family
waiting   gloved hands over lips saying
my beige linen suit   would have better covered
my lineage.   I give them plenty   to wag their heads over.
For Holy Matrimony   I stand firm on the Catholic Church.
My Quaker William   pledges the souls   of our unborn
children   into the Church's care.   Absent   *Father's Name*
on my Baptismal Certificate   an early morning
wedding shorn of Mass   a small group.
His witness   a boyhood friend   keeps calling him
Chicken.   Tante Elsa   up from New York
stands with me.   Such joy   to be far
from that city   Mrs. S's poison tongue.
William's love   like a spring shower   washes
the soot from the air.   He will take up his post
as lighthouse keeper   take me to live
in a white clapboard house   next to hope's beacon.
I own   it is not displeasing   to move out of town
put the island's scant expanse   between us
and his family.   Feeling so fine a bride,
though my dress is thin   for an island spring.
Outside the church   a raw wind   an early daffodil.

                              Amelia
                           35 years old
                       Eastern Point Lighthouse
                   Gloucester, Massachusetts, 1927

   TALLY

   We talk about our lighthouses   the head keeper's wife
   and I.   Mine are tallied by babies   Ruth born last
   at Gurnet's Point   where supplies were rowed
   across the harbor.   Margot made her entrance
   one icy night   at Minot's Ledge
   and Doris at our first light   Sankaty.
   My father-in-law   rode out in his wagon
   with our groceries.   Here at the Point
   I feel blessed   with indoor plumbing.

   Today we sit in my kitchen   mending
   on our laps.   Through the rain-splattered window
   lighthouse becomes   Eiffel Tower.   I dig out
   my Grand Tour jewelry   from a steamer trunk.
   Pins and necklaces adorn   our house dresses.
   She asks about New York   my life.
   I say the parlor was large enough   for a grand piano
   where I learned to play.   My fingers dance
   on my aproned lap   knuckles raw.
   At the sink   looms the washboard
   where I learned to scrub.

Part II Notes

5.   *Penny Candy*

In 1896, Leo Hirshfield of New York introduced the Tootsie Roll, using his daughter's nickname, Tootsie.

6.   *To My Daughter Amelia I Leave*

In 1909 the wages of an unskilled female worker were $2.50 to $3.00 a week, or up to $120 a year, less for live-in domestic workers. The purchasing power of $100 was equal to $2,637 today. The average cost of a house was $2,750 in 1912.

7.   *The Grand Tour*

By custom, elite young men (particularly British) in the 16th and 17th centuries undertook a European tour of cities which could last for a couple of years. Young women of equal means, or those of either sex who could find a sponsor, would also make the tour, whose purpose was to take in the culture of classical antiquities. The French Revolution in 1789 effectively ended the tour, and then railroads of the 19th century changed tourism. However, the big European trip was still thought of as The Grand Tour.

8.   *Follies*

The New Yorker Staats-Zeitung German newspaper was founded in New York in 1834. It claims to be the leading German-language weekly in the United States today.

9.   *One Last Burden*

The Spanish Flu epidemic of 1918-1919 was the deadliest influenza pandemic in history, killing some 20-50 million people worldwide, including 675,000 Americans. Spain was particularly hard hit, thus the name Spanish Flu. More U.S. soldiers died from the flu than were killed in World War I. As the pandemic worsened, people died within hours or days of contracting it. The New York City Health Commissioner tried to slow transmission by ordering businesses to stagger their work hours to avoid overcrowding on the subways.

Quebec, Canada

San Fernando, California

PART III

1931-1949

Azores Islands, Portugal

Gloucester, Massachusetts

Westfield, Massachusetts

Nantucket, Massachusetts

The future belongs to those who believe in the beauty of their dreams.
— Eleanor Roosevelt

Eleanor Roosevelt (1884 - 1962) was a new kind of First Lady who carved out a role for herself as an independent woman active in public and political life. She was an advocate for human rights, civil rights, and women's rights.

Ruth
6 years old
Gloucester, Massachusetts, 1930

Beach Glass

All summer I search the small rocky beach inside the breakwater, and Raymond's Beach, too, when Mother takes us there. My eyes can pick out beach glass from under a stone. I look for rounded pieces the size of a dime or a penny or even a nickel. The waves haven't tumbled the big ones enough to turn them into treasure. Blue and red are precious. I have three blue and one red. Mostly I find green, brown and white. Tante calls them gems from a mermaid's lost necklace. Their colors go milky in the sunlight. My sister Margot tries to trick me into telling her what I'm doing. If I tell her they're Mama's birthday present, she will hunt for them, too, give hers to Mama first.

                                        Amelia
                                     38 years old
                            Gloucester, Massachusetts, 1930

Beach Glass

I come into the kitchen to make breakfast   find Ruth up
before her sisters   first to give me my present
a box of beach glass.   Now I know why she's been poking
along the edge of the water   like a shore bird   all summer.
We turn the glass out on the table   admire this bounty
arrange the pieces   spell our names.
We count them   thirty-eight gems   for my thirty-eight years.
Between thumb and forefinger   the glass
is like satin.   My own edges   can still cut.
We drop them   one by one into a glass-stoppered
medicine bottle   add water to bring up the colors
set it on the sunny windowsill   above the sink.
I turn it   just right   to highlight the one
red piece   like a ruby   my Ruth.

Amelia
40 years old
Gloucester, Massachusetts, 1932

Brownie Camera[10]

from William at Christmas   so his parents can see
their grandchildren grow.   I don't know how
to hold the red box   wind the knob   center the film.
I hate to make the children   hold still   peer at them
through a lens.   The first snapshots have notes.
Hello! Mother has dressed me up in my Easter
outfit—I must be careful not to scuff my shoes.
Hugs from your little Ruth.

When I lose myself   I find each child
in her own frame.   Doris riding her father like a pony.
Margot posed on a rock   bent knee clasped.   Little Eddie
skinny as his fishing pole.   Ruth staring at me   blunt-cut
hair and bangs   thin face   eyes dark with questions
I cannot answer.

                                        Amelia
                                     41 years old
                            Gloucester, Massachusetts 1933

SAFELY MARRIED

Our fifth child comes.   I am heavy with weakness.
His three sisters converge   on our lighthouse.

Fifteen years ago   was I thinking of the fruits of love?
I stepped off the gangplank   safe on William's shore.
I remember standing straight   in his father's Quaker gaze
touching his mother's hand   she   like a songbird
alighting in any choir loft on Sundays   her nesting days done.
His sisters' eyes   struck sparks off the older woman
arrived from New York   said her father was dead.   Yes
when motherhood came   I gave thanks
even with no running water.

Today they spell out ways to avoid   more babies.   I clap
my hands over my ears.   William is a man of hard work
an evening's game of rummy.   I swallow my distaste
for cards.   Here are the sisters   shuffling the deck.
They turn up a card   call it God's game of chance.

I talk to Father O'Riley.   William waits in the car
outside St. Mary's.   At the usual striking of the clock
I take Doris to our bedroom   move William with the boys.
In the cold house   words harden in our mouths
like lumps of coal.

Amelia
42 years old
Gloucester, Massachusetts, 1934

ABSENCE

I lay my head on Tante's lap   let myself be
a nine-year-old again   under the comfort
of her long fingers stroking my hair.   We talk
of Mama   how she withered   until the ulcer bled
the life out of her.   But also   how she left us
her biggest smile on Mondays   when she boarded
the train back to Mrs. S.   My tears   soak the apron
Tante has already tied   strings wrapped twice
around her thin waist.   I tell her about losing
the five thousand dollars   that had become
so much more   before the Crash[11].
How I could never bring myself   to touch
that money.   I intended it for the children.
Even in absence   it stings.

Ruth
12 years old
Gloucester, Massachusetts, 1936

MOTHER TELLS US WHO WE ARE—

my two older sisters, two younger brothers, and me—like parts in a play. Doris is oldest. She reads books, would prop one open at the dinner table if Mother would allow it. She's the Smart One, wants to be a nurse. Margot can get lost bicycling to the tennis court with our friends. I have to double back, listen for her voice, find her pedaling along to "Daisy, Daisy, give me your answer, do."[12] She's the Artistic One. I guess that's why Mother pats my shoulder when Margot wears the blouse I have washed and ironed. Tante makes her give it back as she found it. She's really Mother's Tante. I'm glad she lives with us. Eddie knows the lines to give Mother. When he sneaks the skiff to row Tommy out on the waves beyond the breakwater, Mother understands her Dear Boy is only playing. Tommy is The Baby. He's got Mother calling me Ru-Ru. Tommy doesn't know what a play is, how you've got to have a part.

Ruth
13 years old
Gloucester, Massachusetts, 1937

Reading Stone

I can count on the shape and feel of skipping stones in my palm, their little splashes when I send them running across the water. I can run down the half-mile breakwater of rough granite blocks, my feet sure of their mounds and cups, but I can't be sure of Mother and my sisters.

This afternoon at the beach I bled. Without even a grain of gossip about *that time of the month*, I thought something inside me broke. My sisters didn't let me in on it, and Mother never broke it to me.

Back at home Mother holds out her gold watch. She places it on my palm like on rainy days when we open her treasure chest. I can never untangle the curlicue of her initials across the cover. My fingers fold around it, but I can't feel the story inside. Not like reading stone.

Ruth
14 years old
Eastern Point Lighthouse
Gloucester, Massachusetts
September 21, 1938[13]

Beacon

Mr. Hay, the head keeper, knocks. A hurricane is blasting up the coast. Daddy and I head for his ham radio, but we only hear static. As night falls, the pounding of wind and water grows louder. All of us huddle around the kitchen table with Mother and Daddy. I look out the window at a strange darkness.

The flashing light at the end of the breakwater is out. We press around the window, hoping it will flicker back on because we know what this means. Daddy will have to go out and light the backup oil lamp. Mother helps him with his yellow slicker. Her tight face makes my tummy hurt. My small *Be safe!* comes out a whisper.

We keep our eyes peeled, must be an hour, for a glimmer of light. We are watching so hard, we gasp when the door opens, and Daddy walks in, dripping. *You're back!* All he says is, *Ayuh.* He warms his hands on the mug of hot chocolate I hand him. Finally he puts it down, and we prick up our ears.

I was barely off the porch when the wind knocked me to the ground. I crossed the yard on all fours and slid down to the lower ledge of the breakwater. I got a good grip on the electric cable and edged along. Sometimes it was all I could do to hang on. About half way out, I warrant, my foot found no granite beneath it. I reached my leg out further and got no purchase. The cable felt slack. Then I recognized the rush and crash of the waves pouring through. There was nothing for it but to turn back.

Tomorrow we'll see what the storm did. It must have been bad to keep him from lighting the beacon. Daddy's a Yankee from Nantucket.

Amelia
49 years old
Nantucket, Massachusetts, 1941

Another War

The Great War's end   brought William to me.
Now the Second War   has stolen him back
pressed our lighthouse home   into Coast Guard
service.   I am sent to shelter our children
with William's parents on Nantucket Island   thirty miles out
to sea. Their back fence is sweet   with honeysuckle
wild with bees. The waters off the beach   sun-flecked
their quiet broken by rumors   of U-boats
running in packs.   My childhood wolves
come back   to haunt me.

Ruth
18 years old
Gloucester, Massachusetts, 1942

Scissor-bird

My sister's bandage scissors gleam. When she puts them in my hand, I hold the still readiness of a white crane—long legged handles, crooked-neck blades, blunt-tipped bill—bent to one purpose. I set my sights on becoming a nurse like Doris.

For the dream of the scissor-bird I wait tables at a dockside restaurant. Steady on my legs, I ply plates of fish, snap up tips. At last I enter training, receive my own smooth-gliding bird, learn to probe bandages with its gentle bill.

Anyone can shake down a thermometer, but when hot and cold wake me like an unlucky wind, my fingers tremble. I curl round a stabbing pain in my belly. Textbook words become my own flesh: abdomen, lower right, finger-shaped sac. I am the sick I intended to soothe.

When I follow the track of stitches, I know all my savings will disappear like a fish down a crane's long throat. No technique of bandaging can heal an empty purse. My dream backs out of the room, turns on squeaky white shoes, and strides down the hospital corridor, starched rustle of purpose fading. I go home with a lifetime skill of crisp-cornered bed making, and with bandage scissors, my name engraved along one handle.

Whenever Mother sees a white crane in flight, she brightens. *Good luck!* My scissor-bird lies buried in a drawer.

Ruth
23 years old
Gloucester, Massachusetts, 1947

Chemistry

I didn't recognize the wavy-haired man giving the groom a playful handshake. My just-married friend, mainstay of our beach-going, tennis-playing crowd, beckoned. (Margot used to be sweet on him, but he called her "the actress.") He introduced me to his cousin, Milt, who looked a little older than us. Milt knew me as one of the lighthouse kids. Then I remembered—he had been a substitute teacher back in high school. (How boring he had been in class, or maybe it was the chemistry.) I must have asked, because he started telling me about his time in the war—all state-side. Definitely not the stuff of wolfish flirting. I didn't want to hear about chemical weapons. Turning away to get back to my friends, I asked him to join us at the beach sometime. He turned up, and here's the smiling photo to prove it. We both hold our sunglasses in our hands, eyes daring the camera not to see two unlikely elements drawn together in a new bond.

Ruth
23 years old
Gloucester, Massachusetts, 1947

More Chemistry

Milt's mother had picked out a nice Portuguese girl for him. Dolores is the first word out of Mrs. B's mouth when we meet. No how do you do. I mention that I know her. My mistake. Oh, how thick and shiny her hair is. Don't I agree? Milt knows what a light sweet bread she makes. Now it's hard to like Dolores.

Mrs. B gets a kick out of starting a sentence in English and finishing in Portuguese to lose me. She pronounces her opinions in English, though. Something unsound about growing up in a lighthouse. Three hundred years of Nantucket Island history? Pff! Now the Azores are real islands! She even dulls the luster of my favorite ring. Informs me opals are bad luck. The funny thing is, Milt never hears the same words I hear.

Ruth
25 years old
Gloucester, Massachusetts, 1949

Fingers Crossed

Mother's duty is done, with Margot's wedding set for July, mine in September. Talk of California starts like a sighing breeze, a few swirl-ups of dust and leaves. Soon a wind whistles under the door and sets our dog Skippy to whining. Nothing can stop her, not even Daddy who has never lived apart from the sea, because Eddie has moved to the Golden State.

She sets her mind to dividing her European treasures. Doris comes up from New York on the train with her four-year-old Bobby. We sit on the floor by the trunk, three girls claiming her jewelry piece by piece.

I pick a pendant with a small diamond, a lovers' knot pin, keep my fingers crossed for her pocket watch. The first time I held it, the lightness in my palm, the softness of the gold surprised me. I wondered why Mother said the watch was too heavy to wear. She slips the emerald and pearl ring on my finger, the one I have tried on at each opening of the treasure chest since I was little. Finally she lifts the watch, dangles it on its fine slide chain. It hypnotizes with questions. Who's it from? Where's it from? Why's she leaving? Why not staying? She loves me. She loves me not.

Too old-fashioned, Margot and Doris agree. Mother runs her finger over the monogram on the cover before placing it in my palm. A couple of winds and the watch ticks to life. I close my eyes, hold it to my ear as though it speaks a language I can understand.

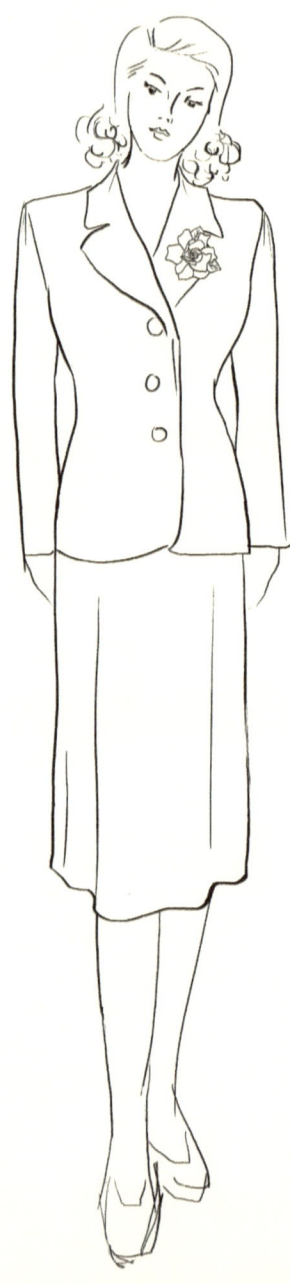

Ruth
25 years old
Quebec, Canada, 1949

Honeymoon

The ceremony, shower of rice, Tante urging a sandwich on me—all pass like the morning's rain. "Just Married" soaped on the rear window makes knowing folks in other cars smile. The tin cans tied to the bumper keep up their chatter *honeymoon, honeymoon, honeymoon* long after Milt stops to untie them.

I dissolve into giggles when he parks the car in front of our hotel, the Chateau Frontenac. As in a movie, I walk from scene to scene always drawn closer—from the lobby where I loop the letters of an unpracticed name at an ornate desk, past the Grand Salon and dining room with their French furnishings, up to the turned-down bed of our room. I turn to consider dinner—how elegant my emerald green wedding suit and matching suede purse and pumps will feel in the dining room.

The time comes to slip into my silky nightgown, Margot's gift. I should have listened to her wedding night knowledge. I near the bed like the edge of a cliff. Later in the dark, I retreat to a secluded corner of my mind's Grand Salon. I draw in all the details of armchairs and potted plants for the kind of place where mannerly ladies drink tea, legs crossed, gloves on their laps.

Ruth
25 years old
Westfield, Massachusetts, 1949

DEAR MOTHER,

I'm writing in a park with the sweet name Grandmother's Garden. I like to call it Grandmother Magda's Garden and imagine her planting flowers in the spring, seeking the cool shade in summer. I imagine her light step on the stone paths for company. Instead, a table and bench of slate must settle me, like sitting on the granite breakwater used to do back home. But where is home without you there?

I am learning to sew on my Singer. I made a straight skirt from a Simplicity pattern and even got the waistband right. On Friday after Milt's week on the road, I surprised him with beef stew from *The Joy of Cooking*.

When Milt was away—I can barely write the words—my little dog Dolly who came with me from Gloucester was hit by a truck. The couple next door was swell. They insisted I stay with them, helped me bury her. Milt got me another dog, and I call her Dolly. It's not the same.

The old maple next to me turned scarlet after the early frost. The trunk is so big, I can't get my arms around it. Kind of like marriage.

                              Amelia
                           57 years old
                  San Fernando, California, 1949

DEAR RUTH,

Lovely snapshot—how sweet your little house. We too
are nicely settled—in the house Eddie found. He took
this photo of us—standing by the garage. See the window?
Dad put it in to give me light—for my new
automatic washing machine. The dress I was wearing
the shade of green—makes me look like I'm taking on weight
but Dad stands tall—ever the lighthouse keeper.

I planted my dear black-eyed susans—first thing.
Grandmother Klara planted them by the front door
of our apartment house—a beacon for Mama.
They came up every summer. Remember their sunny faces
by our own back steps—at Eastern Point?

I'm glad to hear you're acquiring—wifely skills. Your sister
Margot is becoming an accomplished seamstress.
As for marriage—if it doesn't grow big—with strong roots
it can't withstand the storms. May you always fulfill
the promise of your baptismal name—true companion
to your husband.

Blessings.

P.S. You will come to love—your new Dolly.
P.P.S. A dog's name—can always be changed.

Part III Notes

10. *Brownie Camera*

Eastman Kodak Company introduced the Brownie camera in 1900, a box camera made of cardboard. The name comes from the brownies of folklore in the Palmer Cox cartoons of the day. The Brownie No. 2 was sold from 1901-1935. The red cardboard model would have cost $2.50, or about $34.00 today.

11. *Absence*

Many people lost their fortunes in the stock market crash of 1929.

12. *Mother tells us who we are—*

Daisy Bell (Bicycle Built for Two), written in 1892 by Harry Dacre, opens with "Daisy, Daisy, give me your answer, do."

13. *Beacon*

The 1938 New England Hurricane remains one of the deadliest and most destructive to strike Long Island, New York, and New England, perhaps only surpassed in power by the Great Colonial Hurricane of 1635. An estimated 682 people were killed by the storm.

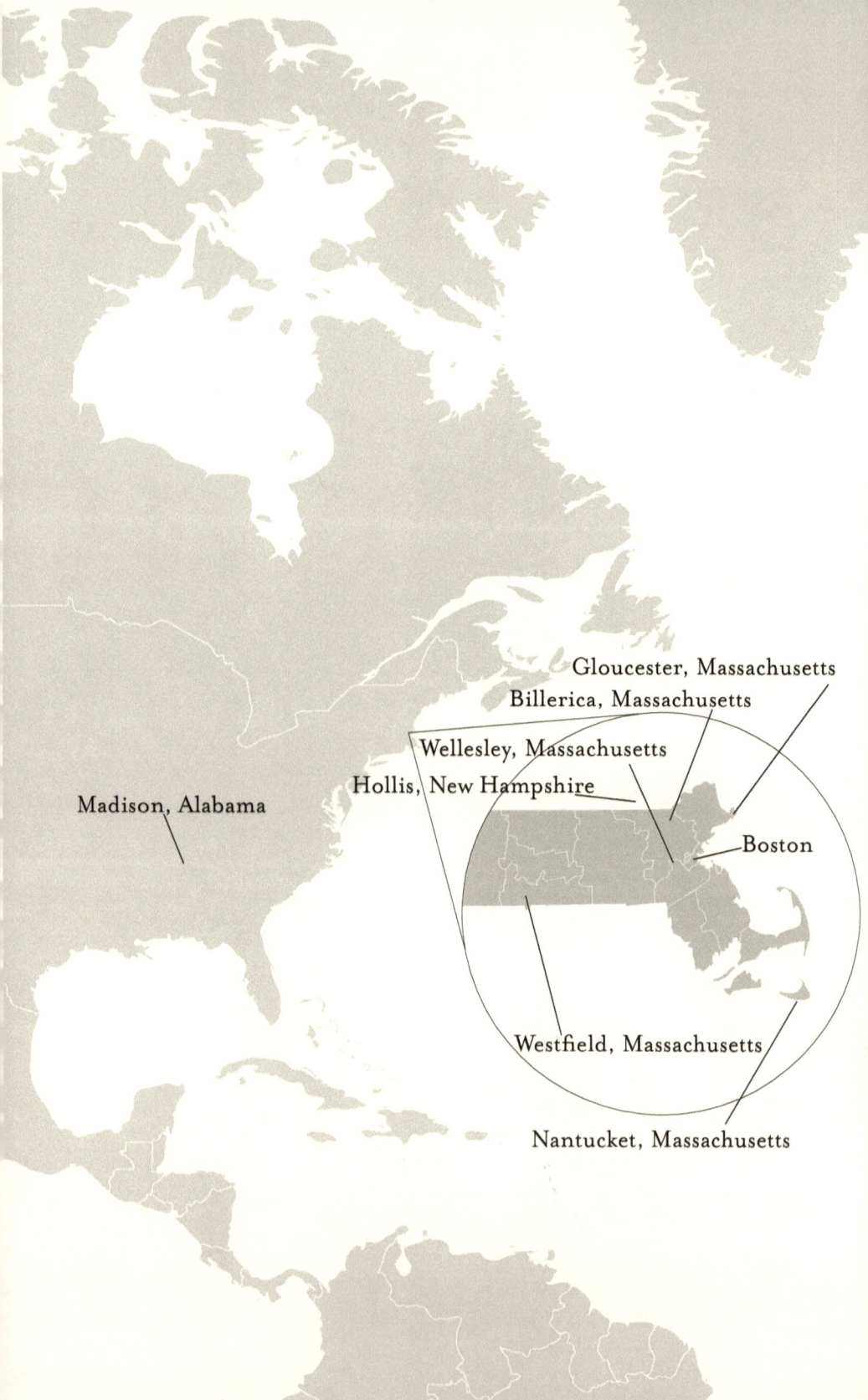

PART IV

1954 – 1990

Azores Islands, Portugal

Barcelona, Spain

Rome, Italy

Each suburban wife struggles with it alone. As she made the beds, shopped for groceries, matched slipcover material, ate peanut butter sandwiches with her children, chauffeured Cub Scouts and Brownies, lay beside her husband at night— she was afraid to ask even of herself the silent question — "Is this all?"
— Betty Friedan, *The Feminine Mystique*

Betty Friedan (1921-2006) co-founded the National Organization for Women (NOW), established the National Association for the Repeal of Abortion Laws (now known as NARAL Pro-Choice America), and, with such other leading feminists as Gloria Steinem and Bella Abzug, helped create the National Women's Political Caucus in 1971.

Nora
4 years old
Westfield, Massachusetts, 1954

Reading Aloud

Down the rabbit hole
with Alice and the white rabbit,
his gold watch just like Grandma's.
Falling, darkness, bad dreams. I am brave
from my seat on the sofa back, my legs
over Mom's shoulders. Her voice
makes the words less scary
when Alice and I grow and shrink.
My fingers twirl Mom's hair
hold tight when the Queen of Hearts
starts her red shouting. Soldier cards
with black clubs come running,
but they will not get me up here.
We are both afraid when
the Cheshire cat leaves his smile
hanging in the air. Keep reading,
I say, so he can't sneak up
from behind the sofa.

Ruth
32 years old
Nantucket, Massachusetts, 1956

We Both Sewed

Misty
the name on the cottage
where I invited my sister Margot
for lunch one stifling island day. While I stood over
hot dishwater, sweat beading my upper lip,
she sat at the table and kept up a patter.
I told her about buying the red straw-hat print on sale
for the skirt and blouse I made. She came
up behind me and put her hands on my hips.
Oh! That's you, not the skirt!
She never passed up a chance to needle me. Already shouting,
I wiped my shaking hands on my apron.
Milt hustled the children away to the beach
with its shushing waves. She was jealous of me,
of us renting the cottage, of having the money.
I screamed at her to get out,
tears mixing with sweat.
Milt passed her on his way back, shook his head,
some people never change. Margot tried to take things
from me. Thrown together as kids,
we were as different as tick and tock. One summer
she got me to wade in and pick pond lilies to sell.
I knocked on more doors, collected more nickels.
She said I didn't deserve more than her
and made me cry.

Margot
34 years old
Nantucket, Massachusetts, 1956

WE BOTH SEWED

Salty
the name on the cottage
where my sister Ruth invited me
for lunch on a sunny island day. While she
did the dishes at the sink,
I sat at the table keeping her company
I told her I liked the yellow straw-hat print
of the skirt and blouse she wore. I went
up to her and put my hands on her hips to show her
the skirt had too many gathers to be flattering.
I might as well have over-wound a clock spring.
She whirled around, soapy water flying from her fingers.
Luckily, Milt had taken the children for a walk
on the beach. She was jealous of me,
that I was Aunt Margaret's favorite.
She spat out everything she claimed
I'd ever done to her. I left in tears.
When I met Milt and the children
and told him, he said *people change*. Ruth turned
against me. Growing up,
we were best playmates. One summer
we picked pond lilies and sold them.
Folks bought more from my pretty
little sister, but I didn't
hold that against her.

Ruth
34 years old
Westfield, Massachusetts, 1958

Reading Aloud

Nancy Drew solves another mystery in Nora's voice while I do the dishes. A ghost. Seances. My mind floats like soap suds. Nora becomes Nancy. I worry about not being in the brick house, waiting for the blue roadster to pull in. Nancy's mother dead. Hannah, the brick. The girl sleuth trapped and pounding on the walls of a hidden elevator. Her friends rescue her. The girl named George thinks fast, not the one named Bess who is plump like Nora. Ned seems like a solid kind of boyfriend, but I don't know enough about him.

Nora
8 years old
Westfield, Massachusetts, 1958

Humpty Dumpty

I like to open the lipsticks on Mom's dresser,
sniff them like pink and red
flowers. The blue gem on her After Five
compact twinkles to me. I rub my finger
across the waxy perfume, touch behind my ears,
like she does. The top right dresser drawer
holds boxes of jewelry from when she was young.
I never get tired of opening them with her.
I like the charm bracelet best. What would I see
if I could peek through the tiny binoculars?

I shouldn't sneak into her dresser,
but I can't resist the box with Grandma Amelia's
round gold watch. When I open it, I can almost taste
its metallic smell. With my thumb,
I click the case open, pretend I'm Grandma
checking if I am late. What time is it
in California? I snap it shut. At Christmas,
her *God bless you* travels over the telephone
lines all the way to me. It feels like a sign
of the cross over my head. I press to open the watch
again, but it slips from my palm,
hits the wood floor hard.

The cover is twisted back, the crystal
cracked in two. The bent gold hands reach
toward me. When I look up, Mom is standing
in the doorway, arms full of laundry.
I hold my breath. She stares at the floor,
then puts the watch with its pieces
back in the box. Opening her scarf drawer,
she piles silky mounds over it. She never
says anything, never looks at me. I wish
for a word to put us back together again.

Nora
9 years old
Westfield, Massachusetts, 1959

The Heart's Answering Echo

Even through the screen door
I can see her eyes, the color
of forget-me-nots in my back yard.
She asks about my uniform, says she would love
some Girl Scout cookies, but a hard-working
Brownie Scout must need a break. We sit
at her kitchen table with ginger snaps and milk.
Is this what it's like to have a grandmother?
Her two collies, Rocky and Laurie, wag
their tails hard. If they jumped up,
they would be bigger than me.
They are her only children.

I walk up through the "woods" to Mrs. G's house
lots of days after that. Sometimes we have
after-school donuts and watch birds right outside
the kitchen window on a shelf Mr. G made.
We sit very still so they won't fly away.
She teaches me names—indigo buntings,
evening grosbeaks, shows me their fat beaks
for eating seeds. In winter black-capped
chickadees cling to pine cones she fills with suet.

If she has chores, I sit cross-legged
at her bookshelf reading *Bambi*,
or go down cellar and watch Dad,
not her father, but Mr. G's.
He makes old clocks run like new.
First he takes them apart. His workbench
is full of hands that look more like pointy fingers
and gears with sharp teeth.
I tell Mrs. G I like the winding keys best.
They look like hearts.

Ruth
35 years old
Westfield, Massachusetts, 1959

Milestones

At twenty-six, on the eve of my baby's birth, I turn and hold the Kodak's eye, a cigarette raised between my fingers like an exclamation point,

which multiplies into clothespins pricking up from the line like rabbit ears—my fingers red with wet and cold. Steam from freshly washed diapers thins into fall air, clouds the kitchen where bottles boil because formula feeding is best.

Nora's little fingers grasp a stuffed bunny by its ear when Milt snaps the photo he will carry in his wallet. Our little bunny curls on the crib mattress wedged across the back seat of our '49 Pontiac. She sleeps away the miles, Gloucester-bound, sucking her thumb.

Three-year-old fingers curl in mine at Sunday Mass. She looks to me for when to kneel, when to stand, when to move her lips.

Then she's pointing at me. Insisting—she doesn't need me to walk her to kindergarten. Correcting—the place we get books once a week is not pronounced *liberry*.

And now the day comes—when her fourth grade teacher says no one lives at the North Pole. And the morning—when I, fingers dripping dishwater at the kitchen sink, have to tell her about Santa. And the moment—when her fingers swipe her cheeks before the school bus comes.

Ruth
36 years old
Westfield, Massachusetts, 1960

Noon Air Raid Siren[14]

I jump at the screech from the tall pole across the street—so unlike the whistle buoy of my lighthouse girlhood. That warning sound on foggy nights saved ships from staving rocks—lulled me to sleep with a lowing we called Mother Ann's Cow.

Now, down cellar, I smooth the iron again over the sleeve of Milt's shirt. The TV screen rolls a few times before *Love of Life* catches and carries on. Are my children hiding under their desks at school? Did I put an opener in the cupboard for the supply of canned goods?

Sunlight leaks between curtains at the high well windows—curtains I made from heavy fabric. They say to take shelter in the cellar in case of nuclear attack.

Daddy once told me it's the water trapped beneath the surface that makes the mournful buoy whistle.

Nora
11 years old
Westfield, Massachusetts, 1961

Portuguese Blue

I wish we lived in Gloucester
where Dad and Mom grew up.
I could play with Rosamaria Caramona
who has brown hair and eyes like me.
She lives next door to my vô.
We would paint our house Portuguese Blue,
the color of sky and water and sun and happy.
I don't feel dove gray like the Nantucket houses
on one side of Mom's family, or Swiss
like *Heidi* on the other.
I'm happy in the car all the way to Vô's house.
I want to speak Portuguese like him. Dad says
his Portuguese is terrible. I know his English
isn't good, but I don't care. Mom says
there could be a fire in his kitchen
from all the grease on the stove. She says
he drinks. I don't know why Dad gets mad
when he finds Vô asleep on the couch.
Maybe he misses my vovó. She died when I was two.

He calls me Shubee when I roll cigarettes
at the kitchen table with him. In the mornings,
he lets me stand next to him at the bathroom sink
and glob shaving cream on my cheeks.
He gives me a razor without a blade
so I can pretend I am shaving with him.

Dad tells how Vô ran away from home
when he was a little older than me.
Since he lived on an island called Pico
in the Azores, he had to stow away on a whaler.
When it reached America, he jumped ship
in the first port. I love to imagine
jumping ship and finding my way to Gloucester.
Vô used to be a fisherman like Rosamaria's father.
I wish I had a name like Evelina M. Goulart
that Dad would paint on the stern
of his blue and white fishing boat for good luck.

Ruth
39 years old
Westfield, Massachusetts, 1963

Until It Wasn't There

Words curl in my throat when it's time to speak of monthly blood with Nora. I buy a kit with a pamphlet, but put off giving it to her until the evening she comes to me. Her shifting gaze reveals what she already knows.

It's the same look as when she broke Mother's watch. No secrets fell out when it slipped from her hand, yet behind her eyes she had pulled down a shade. I couldn't speak then either. Something inside me broke with the watch. I shut the cover as best I could, put the dented watch with the crystal fragments back in the box, pushed it into the corner of the drawer, buried it with scarves until it wasn't there.

Cradling the watch in my hand on a dark day used to send me back to running and swimming at the beach, fishing off the breakwater—back to before monthly periods brought cares. Before Mother moved away. Before we left Gloucester.

When Nora dropped the watch, there was nothing left to hold on to. Even my breakwater with its ten-ton blocks, when battered by the hurricane of '38, broke.

Ruth
40 years old
Westfield, Massachusetts, 1964

In Goodwill

A peek underneath tells me it is oak. I pay ten dollars for the round table painted white, a heartfelt spray of gold around the edges. I strip it down to bare wood, sand it fine. Its soul is pure honey.

My friend Helen and I sip tea at that table, my tan and her freckled legs outstretched. We joke about "baby flu" after I find out "expecting" is what laid me up in bed. We do not joke about Milt blaming me.

I whisper to her how, more than any embrace, I crave the Atlantic surf drying on my skin, how I lose my bearings far from the lighthouse beacon.

I complain that the brushes of *house* and *wife* keep painting me over like someone's old table—colors of good will, but not my colors. So much stripping and sanding.

A hurricane can gather in my soul. Then my words go gale force, but it's the silence at the heart that tears up the children. I am sorry to see them curled tight as storm-furled sails. At dinner they can barely navigate my Goodwill table.

Nora
15 years old
Westfield, Massachusetts, 1965

The Dance Development

Lights dim for the last dance, always a slow dance, when the cross-eyed boy asks me. The eyes that I search to meet are brown, brown hair glances his face. He doesn't smile when he asks, nor do I when I say yes to my first dance with a boy all evening. He holds me with the flush of success, and his arm feels good around my waist. I crook my arm, light on the shoulder of his sports jacket, and peer out, scan as we turn for who's looking. His hand clasps mine, warm. I don't want "She Wore Blue Velvet"[15] to come to its final sigh. Then lights come up too bright, force our eyes down. The painted lines on the scuffed gym floor divide us without a word.

Ruth
43 years old
Westfield. Massachusetts, 1967

STONE

I grab the receiver and breathe out *hello*. My tummy tightens. Mother never calls. I hear three words before I have time to ask: *Dad has leukemia*. They fall on me and shatter. Something about the slow kind. Daddy taking it in stride. God's will. Rosaries. I sob. She is sorry. I want to say she cannot possibly.... But then I feel a heavy sinking. The same stone that she carries in place of a father.

Nora
18 years old
Westfield, Massachusetts, 1968

Questions for a Grandmother I Have Never Met

I learned to read with Dick and Jane[16], followed
their word-trails to Grandmother's house.
Like her, you had white hair and glasses.
In photos. Why couldn't I follow my letters
to your house?

I have visited your last lighthouse, lone occupant
of a rocky spit. Did the wind wear you to its language?
For comfort do you recommend fog or foghorn?

Some nights you must have looked out
at the flashing guidance to incoming ships.
Was each pulse your *mayday mayday mayday*?

After years as a lightkeeper's wife,
did your wardrobe wear thin? Is this why
you stayed home?

For photos, you pulled your hat down low,
offered your profile to the camera.
For keeping secrets, do you suggest a cloche
or a hat with a wide brim?

Did you smile to discover that your Brownie camera
let you stay on the silent side of the telling lens?

Ruth
45 years old
Westfield, Massachusetts, 1969

Coming Back

May's green leaves hang listless along weary streets. Milt keeps saying he will be waiting for me. I nod. On my back, I follow the ceiling stains to the operating room.

Ruth! Ruth! Daddy is calling me back from the edge of the rocks around the lighthouse. I turn to run to him, but my feet are heavy. *I'm coming!* Blinking against the sun's glare, I make out the doctor's grave face looking down at me. *We thought we were losing you.*

June turns me outdoors to tidy the flower beds, their fresh pinks, blues, yellows muddled by weeds—muddled like me before the hysterectomy. I feel scoured clean. When the '54 flood drowned my photo albums, I had to pry pages apart to peer through the frames of their murky windows. I searched for the day I learned to ride a bike, for Daddy painting the lighthouse from a hanging platform, for the wedding guests on the lawn with sandwiches and cake. All of them gone and part of me silted over. Now, with every breath, I am like a catboat racing across the harbor, white sail puffed, tacking against yesterday and tomorrow for today's wind.

>   Nora
>   19 years old
>   Barcelona, Spain, 1969

BARCELONA APOLLO

July 21
balmy evening
with friends
sated on paella
pitchers of sangria
first-time headiness
gravity defying
walk to the dormitory
commotion in the lounge
students crowd before a small box TV
Apollo 11^{17} someone says
a certain Apollo Ramón
springs to mind
I sink to the floor
two astronauts bounce
like kids on the moon
gritty image, grittier voice
subtitles in Spanish
this sublunar body
itself a traveler
too tipsy
for awe

Nora
19 years old
Westfield, Massachusetts, 1969

The Dance
Variation

In high school typing class, I felt all electric
next to the lead guitarist of a band that played
Friday nights at "Y" dances. We never dated,
but on graduation night, we necked in his pickup.

He hears I am home and drops by to see me.
I come down to the kitchen where a faded
guy in jeans sits at the table, a guy who has been to Vietnam
and back, who has long hair and a receding hairline,
whose teeth were never good. He reads me like a clock
and is out the door within minutes. Now we know
how to cut and run.

Amelia
78 years old
Modesto, California, 1970

Adrift

Back still straight   as Grossmutter taught   I sit
at the window of a mobile home   our final post.
Eddie has cut me adrift   again
this neighborhood   lonelier than our remotest lighthouse.

The time he broke   with his wife and children
he abandoned me next door.   Never a goodbye.
I picked up   followed.
My hands   errant heart-ends   would not hold
five grandchildren to me   but kept reaching
for my dear boy   who is ever leaving.

My bones decree   my moving days are done.
I read my prayer book.   William has turned to golf.
My waist   ahh   thickened
under button-down house dresses
my hair gone white.   I have journeyed
twenty years   from our last lighthouse
left three girls back East   who would have dropped by
brought a pot of soup.
I might have made   Tante's German noodles
but I chose Eddie   who
like my father   eludes me.

Ruth
48 years old
Westfield, Massachusetts, 1972

How a Mother Bites Her Tongue

The Letter

Dear Nora,

Seeing a tree heavy with golden pears on your drive into Rome, eating tiny string beans in olive oil and lemon as your first meal—all so different from home. I look forward to reading more of your adventures in a city I have only seen in movies. How are you getting on with the children? It's nice that you are treated as part of the family.

We are fine. Helen says *Ciao*! Did I spell that right? And raise your wine glass to her. Tonight we are having chicken soup for supper. Yesterday I baked bread, which will go well. We plan to visit Paul at college this weekend. Danny isn't excited about leaving his friends for the day, but looks forward to seeing his big brother. He misses his big sister, too. Send him a postcard when you can.

The Words Bitten Back

I still don't understand why you are in Rome. We sent you to a good college. The one you set your heart on. You studied the mother tongue of Fernando Lamas[18]. For four years. Now you live near the Colosseum, have taken up the language of Marcello Mastroianni. I suggest you throw three coins into the fountain and make a wish. Because that's what you need: luck. I ask myself why you didn't go straight to a good job as a school teacher. Some months your father and I struggled to rub two coins together to give you that fancy education. Did you know your summer study in Barcelona was a gift from Miss Helen? We had high hopes for you. But then you became a glorified babysitter. Au pair. You never even liked babysitting.

Ruth
50 years old
Nantucket, Massachusetts, 1974

Home on Daddy's Island

Daddy's people fished these waters, hunted these moors, traded with Indians. They captained whaling ships and paved the streets with cobblestone ballast. Three hundred years ago they breathed the same ocean air that has plumped me up like a girl again.

Retirement has set us free. Twenty-five years in that river valley town, and finally back to the ocean and a shake-shingled house, weathered gray. I convinced Milt to turn the garage into a rental cottage. I can show you the before and after pictures. Oh, I have my proud moment snapshots—Nora in her prom gown, yellow with a white lace overlay, hard as the dickens to sew, or the church St. Patrick's Day float I worked so hard on. But this is more—it's mine.

I had business cards printed with my name—first, maiden, married. In my hand, they already feel like money. My family name is the fabric of history here. Mother carried her mother's surname like a burden. I wish she could see me now.

Ruth
51 years old
Nantucket, Massachusetts, 1975

Family Name

Rain drops pitter against the windows of Aunt's front room where we visit. *This patter nags at me,* she frowns. *Do you know the story of Grandfather Charles? He was a whaling man. So many ports of call, you know.* She winks that naughty wink I don't like.

Back before the Civil War, a couple traveled all the way from the West Indies to deliver their daughter to his parents' doorstep. Her white throat, like a turkey wattle, trembles. *The girl was with child.*

Charles didn't wait long after the birth to set sail. He left Eliza standing on the wharf, their baby boy in her arms. Can't you see her waving until the dot of white sail disappeared?

The old family name fit tight around his neck. What with riding out his own gales and doldrums, the riggings of his Nantucket life fell apart. News finally came that he jumped ship in Hawaii. That girl expected a whaler's absence of years, but she got forever.

Aunt rises sharply. *He never made an honest woman of her.* I follow her swishing, I-Love-Lucy[19] dress, to the back of the house, considering a word for this.

From deep in a closet she digs out a photograph of the woman known as Eliza. Her Grandmother. *She raised my father to carry the family name. Her name was Potter.*

My great grandmother. Aunt's forefinger pecks at the face. I lean closer, searching the shadows. Do I look like her? Maybe the eyes. Aunt's eyes glint. Her tattle-tale cackle straightens my back. Eliza was of a darker skin.

Ruth
51 years old
Nantucket, Massachusetts, 1975

Potter's Field

Today's sunny sky clashes with yesterday's storm. Aunt's voice still jangles as I walk widening circles out from my grandfather's grave. The frost-raised corner of a small stone catches the toe of my shoe. Brushing aside the grass uncovers "Eliza, Mother of Charles." Over my shoulder, the family headstones stand, backs turned. Here, comfort of son and grandchildren lies out of reach.

Did she live alone, as well? Sinking down next to her on the grass, I don't know what to say. Over time, so many sturdy, white Elizas have taken root on this island. Not our Eliza. I try to imagine her walking down a cobbled street, entering a shop, buying buttons or thread. But I can't get past my own Thursdays working at the Hospital Thrift Shop, watching Black women rummage through clothes on maids' day off.

Tomorrow I'll come back with grass clippers and daylily bulbs from my garden. And a spade to work the soil, turn it over and over until it gives.

Nora
27 years old
Wellesley, Massachusetts, 1977

I Am Not Good with Costumes, or,
One-Woman Show with Tragic Flaw

> *If this were played upon a stage now, I would condemn it
> as an improbable fiction.* — Hamlet

The commandment is imprinted on my soul: wear hippie
to Harvard and thou shalt be written out of scenes
by men and women in well-behaved attire.

I learned to fear and revere clothes young, with my mother
wilting beside me in fitting rooms where nothing fit.
Early on, she tried to take clothing me
into her own hands—smoothed fabric across my body,
pinched seams, folded hems, her lips prickly with pins.

The grown-up day I dare to pull back the drape of a fitting
room door, I emerge salmon-hot. No more waist-less
schoolgirl dresses or Sunday Mass wools, my mother
in miniature. No shades of mannered camel or knife-edged
slate bring round the girl I see in the mirror
from committing wardrobe sin.

The salmon suit shows up at my job interview
in a Boston bank and does all the talking.

My full-length, antique cape once delivered
its own monologue sweeping along the streets
of Rome. On the daily stage costumes can whisper
or shout, but must never speak in tongues.
The hands on the banker's watch clutch for numerals
to end the act. If only he could share a stage
with a salmon-suited girl glinting her honest silver.

I bear such love for elegance. But clothes itch on my body
like a foreign skin.

Nora
29 years old
Billerica, Massachusetts, 1979

Let's Hope It Lasts

Matteo wore his pants too high when I met him.
His jokes made everyone at work laugh. No laughter
eased his face, though, in the old photo he shared—
the skinny, bare-chested boy buried inside the joker.

He spoke five languages when I met him,
but one dialect when he got off the boat in 1955.
So many folks trying to leave war-broken Italy,
he almost didn't get here.

But because his mother was born in Argentina
of poor Italian immigrants before the first war,
Matteo's family left Italy as South Americans
after the second. Such are the crossings of survival.

His father took him from the big farm house,
its embrace of grandparents, uncles, aunts, cousins,
traded the tang of manure for the eye-burn
of Boston factory smoke.

Within days of arrival, his whole family had jobs.
Matteo started as a bus boy, moved to short-order cook.
He wanted to be a chef, so he went to high school.
The space age needed engineers, so he went to college.

He was divorced when I met him.
When his parents met me, I heard
a not-quite-sotto voce *let's hope it lasts*.
After all that struggle, they still put their trust in forever.

Nora
32 years old
Hollis, New Hampshire, 1982

So Close to Broken

A gusto for upside-downing marriage and living together
goes flat once we contemplate a child. We come to our
knees before a willing priest to receive his blessing.
On this sunless day, some god of weddings smiles
through the yellow window panes and charges the chapel
with golden light. The priest's voice rolls out the rhythmic

message of Corinthians. *Love is always patient and kind.*
Never boastful or conceited. Does not take offence, is not resentful.
I am so close to broken by the love I want, the words *I do*
break in my throat. The best man's handkerchief is pressed
into my hand. Afterwards, I pose for a seated photo
in my off-the-rack, off-white, street-length dress— some lace,

some tulle, no veil. Lingering resistance to tradition. Nod
to mother's wedding suit. My feet are poised in low-heeled
Spanish shoes. Blue-suited Matteo stands behind my chair
like a traditional husband. Somewhere beyond the trees,
our gazes intersect in the frail future. Again the wedding god
touches us in the yellow reception tent on the lawn, tints

the small sanctuary of family and friends with saffron.
The album pictures will attest the promising light. *Love endures.*
My head resounds, a *booming gong*, a *clashing cymbal*,
with my enduring hunger to be the one beloved. For love
I give away all that I possess, my only self. *Love is never*
selfish. I am quick to offer my husband the first slice of cake.

My heart promises every first slice in return for love.
Its own sticky bargain.

Nora
33 years old
Hollis, New Hampshire, 1983

Unspoken

I say, *a red rash like a butterfly*
painted on my cheeks[20]. We let it flutter
back and forth on the phone line between us,
the wolf-bite of lupus still too raw to name.
If I come to stay with you, I won't know what to do.
Your mother-voice, the one I need to take charge,
blurts an answer to a question I haven't asked.

I want to say you could walk with me
when I have strength, pull up my blanket
when I don't. Make soups that can melt
the cotton in my mouth. Do what you did
when I was a seven-year-old with measles:
bring me ginger ale and toast, fluff my pillow,
turn it to the cool side.
That long ago spring when the red itching faded
and you drew back the curtains on the world
of my bed, I disappeared into books. Maybe
you thought I didn't need you to read to me.
I didn't ask. Now I'm scared, hurt ballooning
at my end of the line.

I hold the string to a lifetime's labor
of forgiving you for not knowing
what to do. Though, maybe it is your
uncertain way of saying, *ask me.*

Ruth
63 years old
Hollis, Hew Hampshire, 1987

Blessing

With three short horn blasts, the 7:00 A.M. ferry pulls away from the dock. On deck, I cover my ears like Nora used to do, shiver under the pale October sun. Puffs of cloud bring to mind the furry collar and cuffs on a warm jacket I loved when I was twelve.

A hot morning in July brought Lara into the world. I promised to visit in the fall. Summer, of course, was high season for cottage rental. My calendar was filled with names, not an open square left. Nora understood. That afternoon at the beach I waved pink streamers for my friends.

Thirty-seven years ago, Nora was born, and I tucked her into the bassinet Mother had left me. I took comfort in the white wicker, knowing Mother had laid us in it. Margot and I passed it back and forth. Now Lara sleeps in it. A nest for each new season of babies.

I am already smiling when Nora opens her door. She wants me to meet Lara. I want to run my fingers over the bassinet. But Nora says she stored it in the attic a couple of months ago. Lara has outgrown it. Oh. I show Lara my gift—a teddy bear that looked pink and soft enough when I bought it.

My hands have forgotten babies—how light, how heavy, how soft, how firm. I perch my granddaughter on my knees, steady her little body with both hands. I want to smooth the fine brown hair on her head, but I'm afraid to let go. My elbows jut out in the long shadows of the short afternoon. The dark season is coming. Thirty-seven years ago I mourned the blessing of Mother's arms around Nora. Now I can't think how to pass on my own blessing.

Nora
37 years old
Hollis, New Hampshire, 1987

The L Word

I wonder why
Lara's baby newness—
become three-month-oldness—
doesn't awaken in Mom
the urge to hug and nuzzle.

Lara's birth awoke in me
the sleeping wolf of lupus,
but Mom's eyes don't betray
a flicker of worry.
No question about chemo,
or relief that I still have my hair.

I plunge in, telling how the cold cap
all but freezes my blood
to keep chemo from my scalp.
(What I don't say:
no such contraption for ovaries.)
I show how I can bend my legs,
so recently like two water balloons.
Proof of kidneys back to work.

She reassures me I'll soon get my figure back
as I did after little Andy was born.

When my first lupus pregnancy ended
in a gush of blood, her words of comfort
included, *It's for the best.*
But also, *Reckless.*
On the third roll of the autoimmune dice,
is she thinking, *Lesson learned?*

Today some hungry wolf gobbles
the light from her eyes
but also the tender word
from her tongue.

Ruth
64 years old
Nantucket, Massachusetts, 1988

Unzipped

Sun gleams on my black Singer, the one I
have used all my married life and still shiny.
I sit at my sewing table to finish a skirt. The
zipper slides from its slim package,

green and limp into my hand. I lay it against
the skirt. Pick it up. It doesn't act right.
Unzip? It yawns open like the letter *Y*. Zip? It
straightens up like an *I*. What do you usually
do? I can't pin it down for the answer.

Nora
39 years old
Hollis, New Hampshire, 1989

Mom in a Once Familiar Place

Her shoes, turned madmen, plague her to put them put on.
Sneakers must replace slippers, moccasins un-foot
sneakers, and slippers vanquish moccasins. A grand satire
of the old family shopping trip for shoes to fit her narrow
foot. My brother and I would wait out the trying on,
the walking back and forth, the choosing, by taking turns
on the shoe man's stool. Back home playing at shoe man,
we'd fit her with pair after pair from her closet. Now Dad
plays the shoe man.

The big hand draws close to the little hand of decline. Mom
is left stranded in a once familiar place holding one slipper,
unsure if she is the girl or the mean stepmother. After a
goodnight kiss, she looks straight at me. *Bolt your door. I
might come up to your room with a knife.*

I thought grief must be tall and grim and dressed in gray.
But it swoops down—flapping, hoarse, and black.

Nora
40 years old
Nantucket, Massachusetts, 1990

Bead by Bead

Two hours and the ferry ties up on Mom's shore.
She stands stiff at the front door. I wrap my arms
around her hollowing body, but her arms are forgetting
how. More and more her own island, she asks Dad
for water, to turn on the TV, to change the channel.
He overcooks the pork chops. At the table,
her back curves, thin shoulders slump. She watches
while he cuts her meat. We chew. Conversation stutters
between swallows and bites.

The next morning she is bright with something to say.
I want you to take my jewelry, whatever you want.
Do it now while I know I am giving it to you.
Go upstairs. Dad nods.

She loved her ivory jewelry—seagull, wings stilled in flight to a
lapel pin, scallop shell for this pilgrimage, heart, plump vessel
of tears. Grandma Amelia's gold jewelry inhabits the same
dresser drawer, different house. Yes, the diamond pendant,
the lover's knot pin, the emerald and pearl ring. I find
the pocket watch in pieces, just as it was put away the day
I broke it. The smell I remember, now know, from my own
body—the faint iron scent of blood. Here lies regret
on a bed of cotton. My broken mother can't be fixed.
I close the box and put it back. Downstairs I show her
what I have chosen. *Get more. I want you to have it.*

I take an ivory necklace, a coral one. They feel like loot,
like finders keepers. I rub the ivory like prayer beads,
each smooth sphere a finding I am bound to keep.
Again I show her, but this time her eyes
are as unfathomable as infants' eyes, without their promise.
The effort of each vague smile a separation, bead by bead.
Her flat voice the string that will finally break.
Losers weepers.

Nora
40 years old
Hollis, New Hampshire, 1990

Husband in Black and White

I'm gonna sit right down and write myself a letter, and make believe it came from you.
— George Young, Song by the Same Title

A second cup of coffee cannot fill this empty morning.
Our mouths churned last night with words, boiled over
with words that now float in a cold and milky soup
of letters. I shut my eyes against your icy mask, picture it
melting in the car, in the office your grief spilling out
on paper.

Dear Nora, you write. No. *Nora, my darling,
No sooner did I sit down at my desk, than I wanted to slip
my coat back on and drive home to you. I keep reading
the words I uttered in every letter and contract before me.
Last night the savage that lies low in me rose up and, as he
once chased his sister with a pitchfork, hurled sharp words
at you. Not one of them speaks true as a single wildflower
carried home to you from a walk in the woods. Tonight
I will arrive with a bouquet of daisies and swear to you
I'm sorry on a snowfall of petals. I will bring champagne.
We will let our bitter words evanesce in bursting bubbles,
toast all that is sweet in ourselves. I lay down my regret
on white paper in black ink, an inscription like the one
I read this morning in the hillside orchard, the writing
of bare apple boughs against snow.*

If only the pen, the paper, the words were your own.

Nora
40 years old
Madison, Alabama, 1990

Souvenir

A card-mounted photo of Grandma Amelia, imprinted
St. Augustine, *turns up months after her death.*

You, sepia-soft, elicit my sharp intake of breath, shiver
of recognition. I have never imagined you young, and now
I grieve for your beauty, soon to languish through the Great War,
packed away like your mold-stained photo.

You do not smile. I grieve because you are a lady's companion,
in service to Mrs. S. Still, I smile looking at your face,
just as some handsome young man in the dining car
must have smiled at you on the train from New York.
I grieve because you looked down, too shy to speak.

You must be hot in your heavy traveling dress, binding corset.
And thirsty, standing there in an orange grove. Did someone
offer you fresh-squeezed juice? I grieve because nothing
will quench like that sour sweetness again.

You wear your hair in a bun at your nape. I grieve because
I don't know if it really is the color of sepia. Your unsuspecting
hands rest lightly, one on the other, at your waist. I grieve
knowing they will chap from scrubbing laundry and blister
from burns at a stove.

Your dark eyes try to hide what Tante Ursula has branded you:
love-child, readable, you fear, as the gold letters on your photo.
I grieve because, to avoid her gaze, you will not go to Doris's
capping ceremony. To be a nurse—once your own dream.

On a distant day, as your eyes follow your daughter Margot,
you will say *I hope that nice lady visits again.* I grieve
because your daughter Ruth's mind—my mother's mind—
will be unraveling as the last threads break in yours.

I grieve because you lived almost one hundred years,
and only now do I love you.

Part IV Notes

14.   *Noon Air Raid Siren*
During the early years of the Cold War and then the Cuban Missile Crisis in 1962, air raid drills were conducted on a regular basis around the country in preparation for being bombed by the Soviet Union. A siren sounded alerting people to take cover in their basements or bomb shelters. School children sheltered under their desks. Many students wrote letters to President Kennedy asking him not to press the button. A common joke during those years was "What do you want to be if you grow up?"

15.   *The Dance, Development*
Blue Velvet (written by Bernie Wayne and Lee Morris) was recorded by Bobby Vinton in 1963 for his Blue album. Other artists recorded it, but Vinton's is considered the definitive version.

16.   *Questions for a Grandmother I Have Never Met*
Nora learned to read with the *Dick and Jane Early Readers Series*, books used in elementary schools from the 1930s through the 1960s, Scott Foresman publishers.

17.   *Barcelona Apollo*
American astronauts on the Apollo 11 mission, commander Neil Armstrong and lunar module pilot Buzz Aldrin, were the first two people to walk on the moon.

18.   *Family Name*
I Love Lucy was a television sitcom starring Lucille Ball that ran on CBS from 1951 to 1957.

19.   *How a Mother Bites Her Tongue*
Ruth mentions two movie actors: Fernando Lamas (1916-1982), born in Buenos Aires, Argentina, signed with MGM in 1949 and played Latin lover roles. Marcello Mastroianni (1924-1996),

Italian film star, won many awards, including for his signature roles in the movies directed by Federico Fellini, *La Dolce Vita* and *8 ½*.

20.   *Unspoken*
Systemic Lupus Erythematosus is a chronic auto-immune disease that causes inflammation in connective tissues, with early symptoms of fatigue, joint pain, and a characteristic "butterfly" rash across the nose and cheeks. It can affect many organs and systems of the body, and is found more often in women than men. In the 18th century when lupus was first recognized as a disease, the butterfly rash was associated with a wolf's bite.

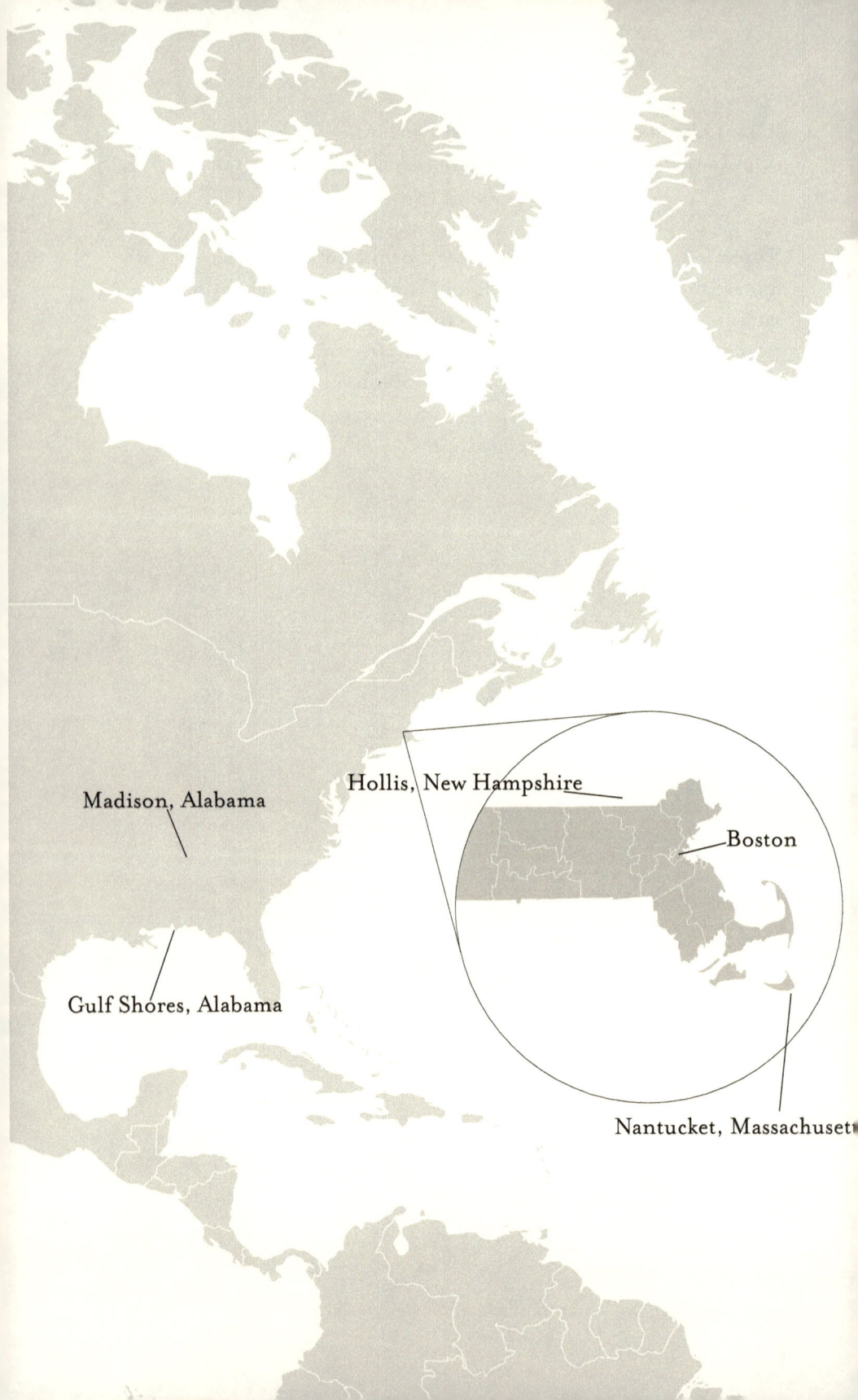

PART V

1993 – 2017

Latisana, Italy

Rome, Italy

So what is a woman's place? For most women it's many places, different places at different times. For almost all women, it's the place of nurturer, whether for the planet or one small creature on it. We learned it from our mothers, both in word and in deed, we teach it to our daughters in the knowledge that they must carry on the culture and care for it. . . . From that continuity they will derive the strength to make their place wherever they think it should be.

— Cokie Roberts, *We Are Our Mothers' Daughters*

Cokie Roberts (1943-2019) was a political journalist who helped transform the male-dominated face of Washington D.C. journalism. She is called one of the "founding mothers of NPR (National Public Radio)" and was a prominent journalist and commentator on PBS television. She is the author of books focusing on the contribution of women to American life, including *Capital Dames: The Civil War and the Women of Washington, 1848-1968*, *Founding Mothers: The Women Who Raised Our Nation*, and *Ladies of Liberty*.

Lara
6 years old
Hollis, New Hampshire, 1993

Adoption

I can hardly wait for the bell to ring.
    Mrs. Ladd lines us up.
She makes us walk slowly
    to the bus and car lines.
Finally I climb into the car,
    and Mom and my brother and me
are on our way. At the SPCA
    the tiniest kittens I could ever imagine
bunch together in a cage.
    We point at the biggest one,
then at the brown tabby,
    laugh at the black one crawling
over the others. Way back
    in the corner I see
the little gray one. I know
    his name—Fluffy.
I have hugged him every night
    for as long as I can remember.

Nora
43 years old
Hollis, New Hampshire, 1993

Adoption

Cats, with their sharp claws, scare me.
I have tried to sandbag the flood
of my small daughter's longing
with half a dozen plush cats, but finally
I give myself over to the torrent
and let it carry me. We land in a smelly room
before a dog-sized cage of too-small, abandoned kittens.
Apart from his sisters and brothers,
a tiny gray one nuzzles the corner—the runt.
Soon he is in the car next to Lara,
her golden brown hair brushing
the cardboard carrier as she whispers to him.
At home she nestles him into a basket
on a folded baby blanket.
He looks lost in his kitchen corner nest.
I bend down to stroke his head, but my hand
enfolds the little furry thing no bigger
than my fist. I tuck him into my apron pocket
and start supper.

Nora
43 years old
Nantucket, Massachusetts, 1993

Ruth, In Memoriam

Final sleep came before first light, left you cold
in a nursing home bed. This morning umbrellas wept
around your grave. Now I look for you in your bedroom, sit
on the bed that has not warmed your sleep these four years.
I face your stolid dresser, once full of mystery, now
a whimper of lost clothes. It needs dusting, but then
it always did. The mirror frames me, as it once framed you.
Helpless, I look for glimmers from before Alzheimer's
fracturing. Your sewing machine. How you made it hum.
My smile caught by the mirror, not unlike yours—the one
you tried on after applying lipstick, dabbing perfume
behind your ears. A kind of rehearsal. I did not yet know
lipstick was for courage, perfume for daring.

Like you, I discovered each day starts with daring
to get out of bed. The rest, a fabrication of courage.
But in my child-mind, you, my mother, in your plaid
Bermuda shorts, sleeveless blouse, canvas sneakers,
were one with the house. Canned pea soup and crackers
on the table for lunch, a lemon meringue pie hot
from the oven, beef stew simmering on the stove.
You were an appliance of the kitchen. Some days
you must have punched for courage, your fresh-baked bread
risen into comfort. Or, courage slipped through your fingers
—a daughter breaking away. The courage
of delight, even in a stiffened voice, words leaning
and lunging like Lara's first steps to your arms.

The dresser hoards half a dozen lipsticks, the coin
of your After Five perfume in its middle drawer. Relics.
I draw Fire Engine Red on my lips, try to smile
into the mirror, but see only a gaudy slash in my distorted
blur. In your blur, each word dropped, mangled, from your
lips, the clearest pronouncement of courage and daring.

Lara
6 years old
Hollis, New Hampshire, 1993

Sympathy Card from My First Grade Teacher

*The wonderful memories of your
Grandma will always be with you.*

I remember going inside the nursing home
    and holding my breath.
I held on to the hard arm of Grandma's wheelchair
    while Grandpa took her for a walk down the halls.

I remember leaving,
    how Dad kicked out his feet
like a clown going down the steps.
    I hung back with Mom.
I wanted to laugh, but couldn't.

Nora
43 years old
Hollis, New Hampshire, 1993

Love in the Time of Gardenias

Snapshots slide from Irene's condolence card,
glimpses of her friendship with the woman
who would become my mother. On my counter,
two twenty-somethings lounging at the beach,
July 1949—Our single days triangles the corner.
A stolen moment of cooks and waitresses
on the back steps of a restaurant,
Our waitressing summer ribbons the bottom.
Mom addresses the camera, head held high
like a WAC[21] returned victorious from the war.

We worked hard, Irene writes, *smoked cigarettes
on our breaks, danced. Ruth met a man
who could dance you to make the room spin.
He asked her to marry him, but he was divorced.
She was Catholic. It ended with a gardenia
pressed in the pages of a book. I never cried so much
with a friend. Your father was not a man
for dancing, but you can see in their photo
he was head over heels. I can still picture her
gardenia corsage at their wedding.*

Each Easter of my memory, she wore a gardenia
corsage on her newly sewn suit.

Lara
7 years old
Latisana, Italy, 1994

CHOPPED SPAGHETTI AND MASHED MEATBALLS WERE MY FIRST FOODS.

I was bursting when my turn came to share
    news with my second grade class.
I am going to Italy to see my dad's parents.
    They have been married sixty years.
My brother and I can say ciao—hello—
    when we get to nonna *and* nonno's *house,*
prego *and* grazie *for please and thank you*
    so we can be polite wherever we go.

At Nonna's breakfast table,
    we drink *cafe latte*
We eat the best *prosciutto* ever
    with bread and curls of butter
at my nonni's anniversary feast.
    And sips of *vino*!
This afternoon, a *gelato di cioccolato*
    with our uncle—*Zio*—at Sandy Bar.
Giggle and repeat:
    Sandy Bar, Sandy Bar, Sandy Bar.

When I'm not eating, I'm tossing crumbs
    to Venetian pigeons in Piazza San Marco.
Italians scatter words—*parole*—around me
    like they have all my life,
just more and faster
    and I can't catch them.
I want to fill my pockets with *parole*
    so I can toss them back.

Lara
8 years old
Hollis, New Hampshire, 1995

Swiss

I've never seen a lion with a curly mane—
      the figurine stops me in the dining room.
Mom says the sad-looking lion
      belonged to Grandma Ruth's mother,
who was Swiss. I used to think Mom was Italian
      like me (she speaks Italian and cooks lasagna)
until I found out Grandpa is Portuguese.
      She's Swiss, too.

MDCCXCII is a date in Roman numerals.
      she shows me how to figure it to 1792.
The words on the base are Latin
      so we go to the encyclopedia,
and there it is—the Lion of Lucerne
      carved on a cliff. It's big.
Mom says ours must be a souvenir
      given to her grandma many years ago.
I point out the small chip on the base.
      She nods, it was always there.
Usually souvenirs make you remember,
      but this one made us find out
about brave Swiss Guards who died
      protecting the king in the French Revolution.

Grandma Ruth kept it in her dining room, too.
      Mom never liked it, but she likes to think about
the hands that have held it—
      her grandma's, her mother's, hers, and now mine.
I don't feel much Swiss in my hands.

Lara
10 years old
Madison, Alabama, 1997

Cat Dreams

Fluffy crouched in the corner of his carrier
    all the way from New Hampshire to Alabama.
Three days of rumbling under him.
    He didn't understand about Dad getting a new job.
When I showed him his house,
    he darted around, nervous, but the house was empty.
I begged Dad not to make him stay outside the first night.
    He sniffed and sniffed for his familiar backyard,
did the only thing that made sense.
    He headed home.

Mom tells about a dog that found his way home,
    hundreds of miles on his animal knowing.
As that dog runs through my mind, he turns into my gray cat.
    Fluffy runs from bush to bush through the moonlight
on flashes of white paws. His tail is always low.
    Leaves crunch. His hair stands on end,
but he is ears-back ready.
    He runs up the nearest tree.
When his heart stops thumping,
    he backs down until he can jump to the ground.

Maybe it's raining where he is, too. He scrunches under a rock
    that sticks out like a too-small roof.
Maybe he's soaked and shivering,
    dreams of curling up, warm and furry, with me.
Whenever he gets hungry he catches a mouse or a squirrel.
    I've seen him do it.
Miles and miles he pads. His paws get sore.

>   But his dreams push him on toward the back porch
> where he will meow and be let in. Then he's bounding
>   upstairs to my bedroom and jumping up onto my bed.
> The best part is laying himself out back-to-back with me.
>   I hold that dream so tight tears leak out.

Lara
11 years old
Madison, Alabama, 1998

Logic

Yesterday in the shower my
      fingers found a hard bump on my chest
under my not-yet nipple, sore
      when I pressed it.
Mom was alarmed so
      here we are at Dr. Z's.
She examines me and laughs,
      Breast bud. The other will form soon.
I picture one of Mom's flowers poking
      up through the dirt. She
looks like she flunked a test.
      I have learned from my friends
that bras follow breasts.
      That means I'm next.

Lara
13 years old
Madison, Alabama, 2000

Doesn't Every Girl?

A blue and gold cheerleading uniform changes how a girl
    walks down the middle school hall.
I tumble and dance for it,
    wear confidence like sparkly hair ribbons.
Go Eagles! lingers on my tongue, popsicle-sweet.
    The other girls lift me to the top of the pyramid.
I stand on a castle that is nearly mine.

At three I teetered in plastic slippers,
    gauzy pink dress, and cardboard crown.
At five I discovered Elizabeth, *The Paper Bag Princess*.
    My head and arms stuck out of scissor-cut holes
in a brown grocery bag just like Elizabeth.
    I marched barefoot to the cave of the dragon.
He had burned up my kingdom, my castle, my gowns.
    No dazzling dress. No sword.
I conquered the beast with brains.
    The book slipped to the back of the shelf.

Now, I think only of walking with the cheerleaders.
    I copy their lip gloss, hair bands, brand of jeans.
After tryouts, squad list posted,
    my friends jump and scream,
then turn into my silence.
    My castle falls, my kingdom burns,
the blue and gold uniform,
    ash in the dragon's fiery breath.
I forgot that every princess has a dragon.
    A brown paper bag
once changed everything.

Lara
14 years old
Madison, Alabama, 9/11/2001[22]

Laws of Geometry

the angle of
        a plane
intersects
        a four-sided polygon

our geometry teacher
        hasn't guided us through
plane geometry when it
        explodes solid geometry

again and again and again
        on screens in every class
even in Spanish
        the translation
does not change the proof
        plane crashes into tower

today I walked into school
        stomach knotted
by a presentation
        for English class

on a book
        solid object I now
hold to my heart

Lara
17 years old
Madison, Alabama, 2004

Prom Magic

The ritual starts after Mardi Gras[23].
    As soon as prom gowns parade into stores,
my girlfriends and I hit the mall.
    We try on armloads of gowns,
take pictures clowning in the fitting room.
    That's just the warm-up.
Soon Mom and I are driving to formals stores.
    I'm getting more picky.
The gown has to be strapless, no poofy skirt,
    either pale yellow or light blue.
Finally, the one.
    Her face lights up,
and I know I look beautiful.
    She turns the price tag face down.
On prom night I emerge from my room,
    descend the stairs, glamorous
and careful in glittery high-heels, smiling at Dad.
    What he sees is dollar signs
and too much make-up.

Nora
55 years old
Madison, Alabama, 2005

Second Chance Shop

I step inside a limbo where unwanted garments hang
with a consigned droop, cast-off in seasonal metamorphosis
like so many cocoons. I wade among long racks of tops,
round racks of pants and skirts. I am not a good browser,
cannot bring my focus to it, so my eyes swim through
purses and jewelry, even shoes that I would never
put my feet into. Then I see the wall of wedding gowns.
Any display of white confections, their various insets
and overlays of lace, frostings of beads and sequins,
sucks me into a billowing cloud of longing.

I never even slipped into a gown before I settled
on a dress some twenty years ago. I make my confession
to the owner who is willing to help me try on an alternate
wedding. We laugh. My stomach tightens. Silk, satin, tulle
could reset marriage. My mock double might swirl
her frou-frou white skirt, flutter up a butterfly effect[24]. Or
I could emerge from the fitting room dressed in regret.
My armpits are wet. There are no gowns my size.
Another customer comes in.
I slip out.

                                          Lara
                                    22 years old
                                  Rome, Italy, 2009

My Roman life

       begins today in a happy haze
of jet-lag. Since the day
       I first pronounced my name,
the vowels have been whispering
       Italia, Italia. I crimped
and sealed my future
       with the Christmas ravioli.

Heels click-clicking
       down Roman streets, familiar
from my fall semester here,
       language ticks into place
like conjugations.
       Terra cotta tiles at sunset
melt me all over again.

       I cross my favorite piazza,
with its crazy-good frenzy
       of human comings and goings,
crescendos of voices jumbling.
       Did Mom once stand here and sigh
over pistacchio gelato?
       Or was it nocciola?

The crowd shifts, leaves me
        standing alone by a fountain
like the person without a chair
        when the music stops,
unclothes a fierce longing
        to stroll away arm-in-arm
with those two far-away parents
        who landed me here.

Nora
60 years old
Rome, Italy, 2010

Venus in the Eternal City

Lara, let's not forget this rainy day in Rome.
How the two of us, mother and daughter umbrellas,
borne along in an alley's polka-dotted flow
into Piazza Navona, washed up at the feet
of the four river gods. You pointed out your trendy pub,
once my hole-in-the-wall trattoria.

Such clicking of cameras all around us on the bridge
to Castel Sant'Angelo. You bore my pontifications
on tourists heedless of the moment's riches—
patch of blue sky, umbrella's abrupt silence,
whiff of old piss, stone balustrade smoothed
by generations of hands, even garlic memory
of pasta at lunch. So much overlooked
when catching the world in shutter-blinks.

Strolling along the river was like old times—
until we reached St. Peter's. Barricades
slashed across the piazza, funneled
the crowd into the basilica.

Years ago, I walked through the door unobstructed—
even hobnobbed with the apostles on the roof,
envying their view of Rome. This afternoon,
with doves perched on those holy shoulders
cooing a chorus of loss, I couldn't
abide the security line.

Delight awaited in a back-street alcove
of rain-tipped cyclamens. Those pink umbrellas
brightened my own Roman winters. And now you,
Lara, are soaring on Italian, making the Eternal City
your own. While I sought the hush of old cemeteries, listened
for the cypresses' whisper at the gates, you step
from the gilt frames of my revered museum paintings
in high heels, speed from classroom to rooftop aperitifs.

Memory frames you as Botticelli's
modern goddess. Paused on a church step
worn concave by centuries to a travertine shell,
you turn from under your umbrella,
a scarfed and booted Venus,
and wink.

              Lara
         24 years old
   Gulf Shores, Alabama, 2011

Opening the Green Paisley Odds and Ends Photo Album on a Visit Home

Her jaw is strong.
        She was not a woman
to color her thin lips
        and blunt nails rose.
The swirling blues and greens
        of her dress are raucous
in the white satin calm
        of her casket. My fingers waver
above her smoothed hair,
        whiter than the shirred pillow.
Turning the photo over reveals
        Amelia, a great-grandmother
until now, free of image.
        October, 1990 reckons our ages
ninety-eight and three.

She moved out west
        when her daughter Ruth
was expecting my mother.
        Twenty years piled up
like the Rocky Mountains
        before Gramma Ruth
got on a plane. She stayed
        a few nights in a motel
near Amelia and William's
        mobile home. Her first
and only flight, her first
        and only visit. A small suitcase,

KLARA — MAGDA — AMELIA — RUTH — NORA — LARA

with identifying strips
        of red tape, sufficed for a skirt,
a blouse, a nylon nightie.

        I know the suitcase,
heavy with miles
        and miles of mother-loss,
decades of daughter-loss.
        I could never carry it.

Nora
63 years old
Gulf Shores, Alabama, 2013

It's as if

my grandmother's watch sighs when Lara asks to see it.
She wants to feel in her hands what her grandmother
treasured, great-grandmother wore. I can't remember
where I put it, become a tizzy of searching—drawers,
boxes, hiding places, call my brothers. The one who lives
in Mom's house remembers reading *We Buy Gold*,
adding the watch to a pile of broken jewelry.
He doesn't know the story of where it came from
or how I dropped it before he was born. He is sorry.
I mourn the watch I never possessed, tell Lara
it was an object of regret from the moment
it was pinned to Amelia's bodice. Still, she feels
a larger-than-watch-sized emptiness. Did the dealer
who bought it know that regret doubled its weight?
I envision his thumb stroking it one last time
before sending it to the smelter where stories
rise like souls from molten gold, waft on years,
settle into words.

Lara
27 years old
Tuscany, Italy, June, 2014

Through the Lens of a Wedding

Up the back of my gown,
    buttons Mom fastens
loop after loop
    with a crochet hook she carried
across the ocean. Through a stone-framed
    window my gaze drifts over wheat fields,
green-on-green checkerboard
    turns into something old,
a memory in red and black,
    the board of a long-ago match
when Dad nudged his checker
    into a square to be kinged.
I wasn't too young to notice.
    He wouldn't own up,
I turned in tears to Mom,
    with her long practice
of looping Dad and me
    back together. Now

she checks on him, reports
    he's drowsing, buzz of honeybees
outside the window, covers
    over his head. Nothing new.
I am thirteen again, cheerleading camp abuzz
    over the final performance.

On a borrowed phone
  I tell my folks the time, but they
arrive late. Dad
  wouldn't hurry breakfast.
Will he curtail a nap?

  White-headed, he emerges
from the gray stone building,
  a dreamer in this medieval borgo,
his suit our nod to something blue.
  From the edge of the wedding lawn
we walk up a rose petal path,
  arm-in-unaccustomed-arm,
his smile enough for loving words
  he has never been one to strew.
Near the front, he drops my arm,
  strides to embrace Pietro,
a flock of cameras blinking.
  I hold my bouquet steady as a staff
until I, too, can reach Pietro at the hedge
  of rosemary, for luck
in our vows, in our future,
  rosemary for remembering
the dancing Dad, the joking Dad.
  The father-daughter root
cannot be divided.
  Let it lie in dark soil.

Lara
27 years old
Rome, Italy, 2014

Bound for America

I'm taking my husband home.
    My marriage bond = hand-in-hand.
My American bond = birthright.
    We ride the rolling wave of plans, high
on the weekly nine-to-five.
    Bound for America = documents = lawyer.
The wave rolls in without us.
    Bound for America = waiting,
standing on our shore, the lap-lap-lap sinking
    our feet deeper into the sands we're trying to leave.
Bound for America = unanswered phone calls,
    hints of dark months, years.
Bound for America = write to your senator
    = go to the head of the line = visa.
We touch down in America
    on the 4th of July. Our dependence
on rules and who rules = humbled.
    Like immigrants.

Nora
65 years old
Gulf Shores, Alabama, 2015

WIFE-HEART

I left my heart on his bedside table beside a book,
my young-wife offering clear, I thought—wordless,
but bright as first crayons. He saw instead a knickknack
misplaced, my heart-shaped offering untidy. So I tied
my heart with a bow around his keys. He saw
not a knickknack misplaced, but silly mischief
with his belongings, untied the bow from his keys,
tossed my heart aside like time wasted. It was no mischief,
just wife-longing. I slipped my heart in his coat pocket,
tossed aside his gloves. Checking his pocket,
he withdrew his hand to consider the contents,
brow furrowed. He set aside my heart and grabbed
his gloves as the greater need. So I burrowed
into my mind's pocket, safe house of the heart.
When I ventured out on tip-toe, I learned to waste no time
on gestures buried long ago behind our old house.
These days he is the one who gesticulates as if sketching
voiceless thoughts or raking for words hidden
in brain-furrows. Though he stretches on tip-toe, words
taunt him just beyond reach. He stumbles through nouns,
shouts verbs. Does he ever search for the words a wife
never stops longing for? Will he utter them before the bright
crayons of thought scribble over his nouns and verbs?
I leave my heart on his bedside table.

Lara
29 years old
Boston, Massachusetts, 2016

Alpha and Omega

With grainy photo
    from pulsing ultrasound in one hand,
phone in the other,
    I leave Mom a message,
Call me—big news.
    The phone rings, but it is Dad's
voice. *L-L-ara.*
    His broken words more broken-up.
Dad, is Mom there? I have news.
    No. Mom. Accident.
What do you mean? Where's Mom?
    Here. Policeman.
A crash. Instant. Texting.
    What! Mom was texting me?
No, it was the other driver.
    Is she okay?
I'm sorry.
    But...aren't these her eyes tearing up in joy?

Lara
29 years old
Boston, Massachusetts, 2016

Untethered

Where did I tuck
        the folded thought
to call you that day,
        before you slipped away

like the balloon ribbon
        from my child hand?
I cried long after the pinpoint of red was gone.
        Now I am that little girl again.

Or the untethered balloon.

No funeral to say when
        to stop holding my breath.
Your final corporeal gesture a hand-off
        to the steel table of science.
Then the kiss of fire
        to your used-up body.

Today I wake up back in my own bed
        for another getting-on day.
But one envelope in the pile
        of accumulated mail
has your return address.
        It bears your latest
between-us cat card—
        unblinking glamor tabby,
one bejeweled paw raised,
        in a wave.

Lara
29 years old
Boston, Massachusetts, 2016

The Sound of Her Name

My tender bud will never stand
    on a step stool wrapped
in her grandmother's smallest apron,
    pour chocolate chips into a mixing bowl,
or crayon *Happy Birthday, Nonna!*
    under two stick figures holding hands.
My little girl will never know
    the particular magic of a story
read in her grandmother's voice.
    Or touch her nose to a flower
in her grandmother's garden
    to learn the name of that sweetness.
My small daughter will never
    share the delight in making up words
to the night music of crickets,
    songs her grandmother writes in a notebook.
Or find the notebook when she is grown.

    I will call my baby Nora,
let grandmother bless granddaughter
    with the sound of her name.

Lara
30 years old
Gulf Shores, Alabama, 2017

His Word

Dad holds out a lipstick tube
       like a fluted, gold-toned talisman,
a straggler from Mom's empty bureau drawer.
       The only word that floats up to name it, *r–red*.
Even his Italian rossetto eludes him.
       He has always hated makeup.
Mom wore colors a shade
       darker than her lips. Never red.
When he objected, she would smile
       her lipstick smile. A quiet act.

I've never seen him cry. Music
       makes him well-up, but not people.
The tide of his tears takes me with him.
       My eye liner smudges. He points
to his eyes, then mine. *Beautiful,* he blurts.
       I don't know if he means with makeup
or without, but I hug him for his word,
       though it stings with old griefs.
He leans on me, and I feel his fear, how it
       makes him frail. All my life the rat-a-tat
of his sharp tongue has kept me dancing around him.
       Blunted, nearly defeated, it rolls out *love.*

Lara
30 years old
Boston, Massachusetts, 2017

Circling the Sea

A wooden cattle-yoke floats on the waves of the sea, tossed this way and that by the winds and currents. A blind turtle rises from the depths of the ocean to the surface once in a hundred years, puts its head through the hole in the yoke. — Buddhist Teaching

A mathematician calculates
    a one in seven hundred trillion chance
two people will meet, fall in love, marry, have kids.

Nora and Matteo meet at her last-ditch
    typing job. Gallons of white-out
don't erase her chances with him to have me.

Ruth has cramps, almost doesn't go
    to the wedding where she brushes off Milt,
She almost brushes him off again. But then Nora.

Between showers Amelia chances a walk,
    meets William, leaves her umbrella somewhere.
Ruth turns up in the middle of five kids.

Maybe Magda's adorable lisp
    is her one chance
for the passion that gives her Amelia.

Tinkle of shop bell. Klara sells a farm boy
    a lace hanky for his mother's birthday.
Johannes' awkward hand brushes hers. Baby Magda.

And so on—swimming back
        through the generations
in a murky sea of zeros.

Yet, here I am.

Toward my own calculus, I offer this:
        In Italy, I go on a date
with a friend who introduces me to a friend

in a group of friends
        who meet in a restaurant
someone suggests in a little hill town.

We talk. We laugh.
        We love. We marry.
Soon another baby Nora.

Life loves to spin us blindfolded.
        Consider the mythic turtle, circling the sea,
homing in on his compass of ancient wisdom.

Into the waves, toss a ring from the Grand Tour.
        Amelia gives it to Ruth
who loves its little pearls and emeralds,

but never wears it, afraid to lose it.
        Mom tucks it away, but now the safe-keeping
is done. Dad holds it out to me.

One hundred years waiting to be worn.
        My blind finger
comes up sure.

Part V Notes

21. *Love in the Time of Gardenias*
The Women's Army Corps, WAC, was the women's branch of the army. It was created in 1943 and disbanded in 1978 when all units were integrated with male units. Women served as mechanics, switchboard operators, bakers, postal clerks, drivers, stenographers, and clerk-typists. Armorers maintained and repaired small arms and heavy weapons they were not allowed to use. A slander campaign was launched against them by angry male soldiers who didn't want women in the army, as well as by other women, accusing them of being sexually immoral.

22. *Laws of Geometry*
On September 11, 2001 terrorists crashed planes into both towers of the World Trade Center in New York City. Another plane hit the Pentagon, and a fourth one, heading toward Washington, was thwarted by the passengers and crashed in Pennsylvania. Almost 3,000 people were killed that day.

23. *Prom Magic*
Mardi Gras, or Fat Tuesday, refers to the celebration of Carnival which starts on the Epiphany and culminates on the day before Ash Wednesday. Brought to North America as a French Catholic tradition, the first organized Mardi Gras celebration is said to have taken place in Mobile, Alabama in 1703. The tradition definitely dates back to 1830. It is celebrated in ethnic French areas, and particularly along the Gulf Coast region with parades and balls. Stores feature colorful gowns for the season.

24. *Second Chance Shop*
A minute localized change in a complex system causing large effects elsewhere is called a butterfly effect. The term is closely associated with the 1961 meteorological work of Edward Lorenz: "Does the flap of a butterfly's wings in Brazil set off a tornado in

Texas?" However, the first appearance of the ripple effect of a butterfly's wings was in Ray Bradbury's 1952 time travel story, *A Sound of Thunder*.

VOCABULARY OF FOREIGN WORDS
with Approximate Pronunciation

GERMAN
Ach (ahkh): oh, alas
Das Neujahr (das NOI-yahr): the new year
Der Schwarze Mann (der SCHVAR-ze mahn): boogieman
Ene mene miste (EENa-MEENa-MISte): eeny meeny miney mo
Fräulein (FROI-line): little miss, young lady
Grossmutter (GROSS-mooter): grandmother
Grossvater (GROSS-vahter): grandfather
Kaffee (KAFF-ee): coffee
Kneipe (k-NI-pe): tavern
Mäuschen (MOI-shen): little mouse
Mütter (MOOT-er): mother
Oma (O-mah): grandma, granny
Schatz (SHAHTS): dear one
Schlummerlieder (SCHUM-mer-LEE-der): lullabies
Spatz (SHPAHTS): sparrow
Staats-Zeitung (STAHTS TSAI-tung): state newspaper
Tante (TAWN-teh): aunt

ITALIAN
Ciao (chow): Hi! or Bye!
Gelato (je-LA-toh): ice cream
Nonna (NOH-nah): grandma
Nonno (NOH-noh): grandpa
Nocciola (noh-CHOH-la): hazelnut
Pistacchio (pis-TAK-ee-oh): pistachio
Rossetto (roh-SETT-oh): lipstick

PORTUGUESE
Vô (Vo): grandpa
Vovó (vo-VAW): grandma

Acknowledgments

Thanks to the editors of the following journals and anthologies where these poems first appeared, sometimes in an earlier version:

Awarded Writers Collection, "Souvenir"
2nd and Church, "The Dance"
2nd and Church, "I Am Not Good with Costumes, or, One-Woman Show with a Tragic Flaw"
Nancy Drew Anthology, "Reading Aloud"
Number One: a Literary Journal, "I Walk Up the Ship's Gangplank" (published as "Bremen, 1883")
Number One: a Literary Journal, "Beacon" (published as "Beacon, September 21, 1938")
Number One: a Literary Journal, "Honeymoon" (published as "Honeymoon, Quebec 1949")
The Museum of Americana, "I Call This Our Once Upon a Time"
The Museum of Americana, "Liberty"
The Museum of Americana, "Noon Air Raid Siren"
The Museum of Americana, "Barcelona Apollo"
The Museum of Americana, "Laws of Geometry"
The Louisville Review, "Making Clothes for Lotte"
The Louisville Review, "Thanksgiving"
The Louisville Review, "Tally"
The Louisville Review, "Mother tells us who we are—"
The Louisville Review, "Humpty Dumpty"
The Pensters Anthology, "In My Love, In My Song"
The Pensters Anthology, "Cat Dreams"
The Pensters Anthology, "Portuguese Blue"

Appreciation

My deepest gratitude to those who read or heard these poems from the beginning, saw their potential, and urged them into their final form: Inklings Writing Group where the first poem was born; Pensters Writing Group where contest prompts grew into poems for this book; thoughtful readers and friends, Glenda Slater and the late Mickey Cleverdon, who always believed in me, but always questioned; my aunt Madeleine Osborne who shared her memories with me; Beth Ann Fennelly, Jim Murphy and Vivian Shipley for their invaluable advice in the early stages through Alabama Writers' Cooperative; Irene Latham for her reading and especially her hints on child's voice; Kory Wells, who never stopped encouraging, but never let me get away with a poem that was less than the best it could be over multiple versions of poems and the manuscript; Kathleen Thompson who helped me understand when a poem can be overloaded; Susan Luther, who urged me to stay true to my vision; Theresa K. Thorne with her talk "Somebody's Gotta Die"; Larry Brooks for his master class on story structure; and everyone who suggested works of literature to guide me on my way. Heartfelt thanks to Negative Capability Press and Sue Walker for years of believing a book would emerge. Finally, I am indebted to Natasha Tretheway for the inspiration of *Bellocq's Ophelia*.

www.ingramcontent.com/pod-product-compliance
Lightning Source LLC
Chambersburg PA
CBHW020109020526
44112CB00033B/1114